United States
Department of
Agriculture

Forest Service

**Northern
Research Station**

General Technical
Report NRS-56

# Urban and Community Forests
# of the North Central West Region

| | |
|---|---|
| **Iowa** | **Nebraska** |
| **Kansas** | **North Dakota** |
| **Minnesota** | **South Dakota** |
| **Missouri** | |

David J. Nowak
Eric J. Greenfield

## Abstract

This report details how land cover and urbanization vary within the states of Iowa, Kansas, Minnesota, Missouri, Nebraska, North Dakota, and South Dakota by community (incorporated and census designated places), county subdivision, and county. Specifically this report provides critical urban and community forestry information for each state including human population characteristics and trends, changes in urban and community lands, tree canopy and impervious surface cover characteristics, distribution of land-cover classes, a relative comparison of urban and community forests among local government types, determination of priority areas for tree planting, and a summary of urban tree benefits. Report information can improve the understanding, management, and planning of urban and community forests. The data from this report is reported for each state on the CD provided in the back of this book, and it may be accessed by state at: http://www.nrs.fs.fed.us/data/urban.

## The Authors

DAVID J. NOWAK is a research forester and project leader, and ERIC J. GREENFIELD is a forester with the Forest Service's Northern Research Station at Syracuse, NY.

# CONTENTS

# INTRODUCTION

As part of the Forest and Rangeland Renewable Resources Planning Act of 1974, the first national assessment of urban forests was completed in 2000 (Dwyer et al. 2000, Nowak et al. 2001b). This assessment used 1-km resolution Advanced Very-High Resolution Radiometer (AVHRR) data (Zhu 1994) and 1990 U.S. Census Bureau (2007) population and geographic data to assess urban tree cover. The assessment concluded that urban areas in the conterminous United States doubled in size between 1969 and 1994 and covered 3.5 percent of the total land area. Urban areas were estimated to contain approximately 3.8 billion trees with an average tree canopy cover of 27 percent.

To update this first report, higher resolution (30 m) tree canopy and impervious surface cover maps were used (from 2001 Landsat satellite imagery and published in 2007) (Homer et al. 2007, U.S. Geol. Surv. 2007) in conjunction with 1990 and 2000 census and geographic data (1:5,000,000 scale cartographic boundary files) (U.S. Census Bureau 2007) to assess current urban and community forest attributes. These results are being published for each of the lower 48 United States to provide information on urban change and state-specific urban and community forestry data.

This report includes information for the following states: Iowa, Kansas, Minnesota, Missouri, Nebraska, North Dakota, and South Dakota.

Data are reported for the state, county, county subdivision, and community jurisdictions. The jurisdictional units used in this report are derived from U.S. Census (2007) geographic data and defined legal or statistical divisions. "County"[1] refers to the primary subdivision within states. "County subdivisions" are primary divisions of a county and are statistically equivalent entities for the reporting of census data. They include census county divisions (CCD), census sub areas, minor civil divisions (MCD), and unorganized territories. "Communities" are incorporated and census designated places, and consolidated cities (U.S. Census Bureau 2007). For detailed definitions, see http://www.census.gov/geo/www/cob/cs_metadata.html (2007).

---

[1]The primary legal divisions of most states are termed "counties." In Louisiana, these divisions are known as "parishes." In four states (Maryland, Missouri, Nevada, and Virginia), there are one or more incorporated places that are independent of any county organization and thus constitute primary divisions of their states; these incorporated places are known as "independent cities" and are treated as equivalent to counties for statistical purposes. (For some statistical purposes they may be treated as county subdivisions and places.) The District of Columbia has no primary divisions, and the entire area is considered equivalent to a county for statistical purposes. (http://www.census.gov/geo/www/cob/co_metadata.html, 2007)

# REPORT OVERVIEW

The information in this report can aid local and regional managers and planners of urban and community forest resources. This report provides urban and community forest reference information and data from the state to local level on the following attributes related to the urban and community forest resource:

- Human population characteristics and trends
- Urban and community land
- Tree canopy cover characteristics
- Impervious surface cover characteristics
- Classified land-cover characteristics
- Relative comparisons of urban and community forests
- Priority areas for tree planting
- Urban tree benefits

Information in this report can be used by urban and community forestry professionals to:

- Understand general land-cover characteristics and urbanization trends at several geographic scales
- Compare tree canopy cover among similar communities
- Determine areas of greatest growth and areas of highest tree planting priority
- Relate urban and community forests to pollution removal and carbon storage
- Promote more detailed and/or locally appropriate urban and community forest inventories, censuses, or field surveys (e.g., i-Tree – www.itreetools.org)
- Establish local to statewide standards related to urban and community forestry
- Support urban and community forestry programs
- Improve urban and community forest management and planning

The remainder of this section details how information was derived for each attribute reported for the urban and community areas. The subsequent state summaries detail the findings for each state in this region. Most tables for each state are not given in this report, rather they can be found on the CD provided with this report or accessed at: http://www.nrs.fs.fed.us/data/urban.

# URBAN FOREST ATTRIBUTES

## Human Population Characteristics and Trends

Human population and population density changes over time, and geographic distribution are important measurements of the urban environment because human populations are an integral part of community and urban forest dynamics. Within divisions of state, county, county subdivision, and community, total population, population changes from 1990 to 2000 and population density are detailed based on U.S. Census data (U.S. Census Bureau 2007).

## Urban and Community Land

Two geographic definitions overlap: "community" and "urban". The definition of community is based on jurisdictional or political boundaries delimited by U.S. Census definitions of places (U.S. Census Bureau 2007). Community lands are places of established human settlement that may include all, some, or no urban land within their boundaries.

The definition of urban is based on population density as delimited using the U.S. Census Bureau's (2007) definition: all territory, population, and housing units located within urbanized areas or urban clusters. Urbanized area and urban cluster boundaries encompass densely settled territories, which are described by one of the following:

- One or more block groups or census blocks with a population density of at least 386.1 people/ $km^2$ (1,000 people/mile$^2$)
- Surrounding block groups and census blocks with a population density of 193.1 people/km$^2$ (500 people/mile$^2$)
- Less densely settled blocks that form enclaves or indentations, or are used to connect discontinuous areas

More specifically, urbanized areas consist of territory with 50,000 or more people. Urban clusters, a concept new to the 2000 Census, consist of territory with at least 2,500 people but fewer than 50,000 people. This new definition tends to be more restrictive than the 1990 U.S. Census urban definition and encompasses many areas typically considered suburban. The 2000 Census definition of urban was applied to 1990 Census geographic data to analyze change in urban land between 1990 and 2000 (Nowak et al. 2005).

As urban land reveals the more heavily populated areas (population density-based definition) and community land indicates both urban and rural (i.e., non-urban) communities that are recognized by their geopolitical boundaries (political definition), both definitions provide information related to human settlements and the forest resources within those settlements. As some urban land exists beyond community boundaries and not all community land is urban (i.e., communities are often a mix of urban and rural land), the category of "urban or community" was created to understand forest attributes accumulated by the union of these two definitions. The "urban or community" term used throughout this report encompasses both urban land and land in communities.

Percent urban land is a ratio of urban land over total land within a census geographic division, and percent community land is a ratio of community land over total land within the geopolitical unit. In addition, changes in urban land and changes in community land are reported between 1990 and 2000.

For each state, Tables 1 through 4 summarize the population, and urban and community land attributes for the state, communities, county subdivisions, and counties respectively (CD and http://www.nrs.fs.fed. us/data/urban).

## Tree Canopy Cover Characteristics

Tree canopy cover is a critical measure of the urban and community forest resource. Tree canopy cover gives a broad indication of the overall forest resource and its associated benefits. To assess urban and community land cover characteristics, the multi-resolution land characteristics consortium's National Land Cover Database (NLCD) was used (Homer et al. 2004, U.S. Geol. Surv. 2007, Yang et al. 2003). The NLCD, released in early 2007, was processed from 2001 Landsat satellite imagery and provides estimates of percentage tree canopy and impervious surface cover within 30-m pixels or cells across the state. The tree canopy percentages in this report are calculated using the land area (not including water) of the geopolitical units derived from the U.S. Census cartographic boundary data and NLCD. In addition to percentage tree cover, four other canopy cover attributes, derived from the same data, were assessed:

- Tree canopy cover per capita—Tree canopy cover ($m^2$) divided by the number of people within the area of analysis.
- Total green space—Total area minus impervious and water cover (ha). This attribute estimates pervious cover (i.e., grass, soil, or tree-covered areas).
- Canopy green space—Tree cover divided by total green space (percent). This value is the proportion of the total green space that is filled by tree canopies.
- Available green space—Total green space minus tree canopy cover (ha). This value is the amount of grass and soil area not covered with tree canopies and potentially available for planting.

## Impervious Surface Cover Characteristics

Similar to tree cover, impervious surface cover provides another piece of valuable information related to the urban environment. Impervious surface cover gives an indication of an area's developed hardscape, which has important influences on urban air temperatures and water flows and also yields information on limitations to urban tree cover. Impervious surface cover also was derived from the NLCD database (U.S. Geol. Surv. 2007). The impervious surface cover percentages in this report are calculated using the land area (not including water) of the geopolitical units derived from the U.S. Census cartographic boundary data and NLCD. Impervious surface per capita is calculated from NLCD 2001 and U.S. Census data.

For each state, Tables 1, and 5 through 7 summarize the tree canopy and impervious surface cover attributes for the state, communities, county subdivisions, and counties respectively (CD and http://www.nrs.fs.fed.us/data/urban).

## Classified Land-cover Characteristics

Land-cover types also are summarized using 2001 Landsat satellite data that were classified with the U.S. Geological Survey land cover categorization scheme based on a modified Anderson land-cover classification (U.S. Geol. Surv. 2007). Land area, tree canopy cover, and available green space within generalized land cover categories vary among communities, county subdivisions, counties, and state. The percentages are calculated from the NLCD 2001 and U.S. Census cartographic boundary data. The land-cover categories defined here are derived from established NLCD 2001 land-cover classes. These generalized land-cover categories or types may not be present in some states.

- Developed—NLCD classes 21 (developed-open space), 22 (developed-low intensity), 23 (developed-medium intensity), and 24 (developed-high intensity)
- Barren—NLCD class 31 (barren land [rock/sand/clay])
- Forested—NLCD classes 41 (deciduous forest), 42 (evergreen forest), and 43 (mixed forest)
- Shrub/Scrub—NLCD class 52 (shrub/scrub)
- Grassland—NLCD class 71 (grassland/herbaceous)
- Agriculture—NLCD classes 81 (pasture/hay) and 82 (cultivated crops)
- Wetland—NLCD classes 90 (woody wetlands) and 95 (emergent herbaceous wetlands)

For each state, Tables 8 through 10 summarize the classified land-cover characteristics for communities, county subdivisions, and counties and state respectively (CD and http://www.nrs.fs.fed.us/data/urban).

## Relative Comparisons of Tree Cover

A question commonly asked in evaluating the urban and community forest resource is, "How does my community compare with other communities?"

To help answer this question, tree canopy cover was compared among the counties, county subdivisions, and communities relative to other areas with comparable population density and within the same NLCD mapping unit (ecoregion). For this comparison, seven population density classes were established:

- Density class 1 — 0 to 38.6 people/km$^2$ (0 to 99.9 people/mile$^2$)
- Density class 2 — 38.7 to 96.5 people/km$^2$ (100 to 249.9 people/mile$^2$)
- Density class 3 — 96.6 to 193.1 people/km$^2$ (250 to 499.9 people/mile$^2$)
- Density class 4 — 193.2 to 289.6 people/km$^2$ (500 to 749.9 people/mile$^2$)
- Density class 5 — 289.7 to 386.2 people/km$^2$ (750 to 999.9 people/mile$^2$)
- Density class 6 — 386.3 to 1931.2 people/km$^2$ (1000 to 4999.9 people/mile$^2$) and
- Density class 7 — 1931.3 or greater people/km$^2$ (5000 or greater people/mile$^2$)

Mapping zones were delimited within the NLCD to increase classification accuracy and efficiency (Fig. A). The mapping units represent relatively homogeneous ecological conditions (Homer and Gallant 2001). To locate geopolitical units within a mapping zone, centroid (geometric center) points of the local governments were used.

For three or more geographic units in the same mapping zone and population density class, a standardized tree canopy score based on the range of values within that zone and class was assigned to each unit. The standardized score is calculated as:

Standardized score = (tree canopy percent of unit – minimum tree canopy percentage in class)/range of tree canopy percent in class.

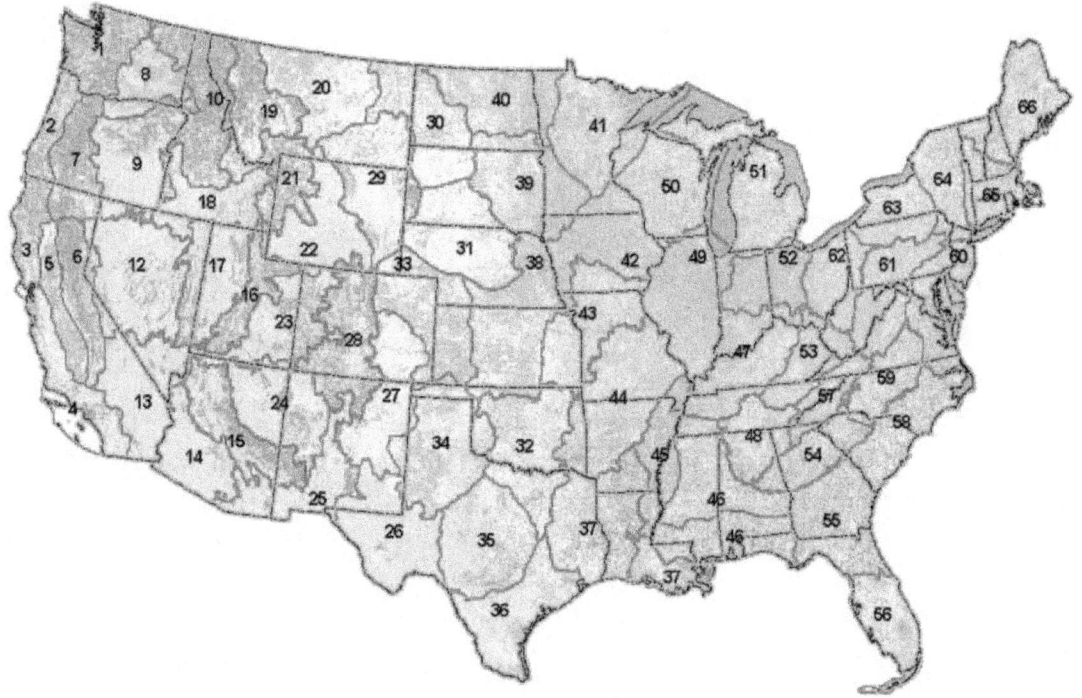

Figure A.—The mapping zones of the continental United States relative to states and land cover (NLCD 2001).

Communities, county subdivisions, and counties were assigned to one of the following categories based on their standardized score:

- Excellent—Standardized score of 0.9 to 1.0
- Very Good—0.7 to 0.89
- Good—0.5 to 0.69
- Fair—0.3 to 0.49
- Poor—0 to 0.29

To help understand the variability of tree cover, minimum, median, maximum, and weighted mean values for percent tree canopy cover in each population density class of each political subdivision are reported in Table 11 for each mapping zone (CD and http://www.nrs.fs.fed.us/data/urban). This information can be used to understand the actual range and values used for the assessment.

For each state, Tables 12 through 14 summarize the urban and community forest ratings for communities, county subdivisions, and counties respectively (CD and http://www.nrs.fs.fed.us/data/urban).

## Priority Areas for Tree Planting

NLCD (U.S. Geol. Survey 2007) and 2000 U.S. Census data (2007) were used to produce an index that prioritizes tree planting areas for communities, county subdivisions, and counties. An index was developed to help identify areas with relatively low tree canopy cover and high population density (high priority tree-planting areas). This index provides one form of prioritization. States and local governments may design their own prioritization method incorporating individual and diverse value systems. The index used in this report combines three criteria.

- Population density—The greater the population density, the greater the priority for tree planting
- Canopy green space—The lower the value, the greater the priority for tree planting
- Tree canopy cover per capita—The lower the amount of tree canopy cover per person, the greater the priority for tree planting

Each criterion above was standardized[2] on a scale of 0 to 1, with 1 representing the maximum population density and minimum canopy green space and tree cover per capita. The standardized values were weighted to produce a combined score:

$$I = (PD * 40) + (CG * 30) + (TPC * 30)$$

Where I is the combined index score
PD is the standardized population density value
CG is the standardized canopy green space value, and
TPC is the standardized tree cover per capita value.

The combined score was standardized again and multiplied by 100 to produce the planting priority index. The tree planting priority index (PPI) ranks each state's communities, county subdivisions, and counties with values from 100 (highest priority) to 0 (lowest priority). This index is a type of "environmental equity" index with areas of higher human population density and lower canopy green space and tree cover per capita tending to get the higher index value.

For each state, Tables 15 through 17 summarize the tree planting priority index for communities, county subdivisions, and counties respectively (CD and http://www.nrs.fs.fed.us/data/urban).

## Urban Tree Benefits

Urban and community forests are important for human and ecological health (Nowak and Dwyer 2007). The benefits ascribed to urban and community trees include:

- Carbon storage and sequestration
- Air pollution removal
- Surface air temperature reduction
- Reduced building energy use
- Absorption of ultraviolet radiation
- Improved water quality
- Reduced noise pollution
- Improved human comfort
- Increased property value
- Improved human physiological and psychological well-being
- Improved aesthetics
- Improved community cohesion

To understand the contribution and magnitude of the forest resource in urban or community areas, the total number of trees, carbon storage and annual carbon uptake (sequestration), air pollution removal, and the associated dollar values for carbon and air pollution benefits are estimated.

Carbon sequestration and storage values were estimated from tree cover (m[2]) multiplied by average carbon storage (9.1 kg C/m[2]), and sequestration (0.3 kg C/m[2]) density values derived from several U.S. communities (e.g., Nowak and Crane 2002). Monetary values associated with urban tree carbon storage and sequestration were based on the 2001-2010 projected marginal social cost of carbon dioxide emissions, $22.8/t C (Fankhauser 1994). The number of urban and community trees was estimated in a similar manner multiplying tree canopy cover (m[2]) by average tree density per hectare of canopy cover from several U.S. cities (Table A).

Air pollution removal estimates are derived from the Urban Forest Effects (UFORE) model (Nowak and Crane 2000) and 2000 weather and pollution data (National Climatic Data Center 2000, U.S. EPA 2008). The UFORE model was used to integrate hourly pollution and weather data with urban or community tree cover data to estimate annual pollution removal in each state (Nowak and Crane 2000, Nowak et al. 2006d).

---

[2]Standardized value for population density (PD) was calculated as PD=(n–min)/r, where PD is the value 0-1, n is the value for the geopolitical unit (population/km[2]), min is the minimum value for all units, and r is the range of values among all units (maximum value – minimum value). Standardized value for canopy green space (CG) was calculated as CG=(max–n)/r, where CG is the value 0-1, max is the maximum value for all geopolitical units, n is the value for the unit (tree canopy cover m[2]/total green space m[2]), and r is the range of values. Standardized value for tree cover per capita (TPC) was calculated as TPC=(max–n)/r, where TPC is the value (0-1), max is the maximum value for all geographic units, n is the value for the geopolitical unit (m[2]/capita), and r is the range of values among all units.

**Table A.—Average number of trees, carbon storage, and carbon sequestration rates per unit of canopy cover for several U.S. cities**

| | Trees | Carbon | |
| | | Storage | Sequestration |
| City | (no./ha cover) | (kg C/m² cover) | (kg C/m² cover) |
| --- | --- | --- | --- |
| Atlanta, GA [a] | 751.5 | 9.7 | 0.3 |
| Baltimore, MD [a] | 598.1 | 12.3 | 0.3 |
| Boston, MA [a] | 371.7 | 9.1 | 0.3 |
| Chicago, IL [b] | 618.0 | 12.9 | n/a |
| Casper, WY [c] | 252.8 | 7.0 | 0.2 |
| Freehold, NJ [a] | 275.0 | 10.4 | 0.3 |
| Jersey City, NJ [a] | 308.7 | 4.4 | 0.2 |
| Minneapolis, MN [d] | 245.5 | 5.7 | 0.2 |
| Moorestown, NJ [a] | 547.9 | 9.9 | 0.3 |
| Morgantown, WV [a] | 829.6 | 10.6 | 0.3 |
| New York, NY [e] | 312.0 | 7.3 | 0.2 |
| Philadelphia, PA [f] | 394.3 | 9.0 | 0.3 |
| San Francisco, CA [g] | 468.1 | 12.3 | 0.3 |
| Syracuse, NY [h] | 583.1 | 10.5 | 0.3 |
| Oakland, CA [i] | 570.0 | 5.2 | n/a |
| Washington, DC [j] | 423.4 | 10.4 | 0.3 |
| Woodbridge, NJ [a] | 557.3 | 8.2 | 0.3 |
| Mean | 476.9 | 9.1 | 0.3 |

[a] Unpublished data analyzed using UFORE model
[b] Nowak 1994a,b
[c] Nowak et al. 2006a
[d] Nowak et al. 2006b
[e] Nowak et al. 2007a

[f] Nowak et al. 2007b
[g] Nowak et al. 2007c
[h] Nowak et al. 2001a
[i] Nowak 1993; Nowak and Crane 2002
[j] Nowak et al. 2006c

To estimate pollution by urban trees in each state, state pollutant flux rates (grams of pollution removal per square meter of canopy per year) were derived from a study of national pollution removal by urban trees for the year 1994 (Nowak et al. 2006d). As pollution concentrations vary through time, the 1994 flux rates were adjusted to 2000 values based on average regional pollution concentration changes between 1994 and 2000 (U.S. EPA 2003). As

flux rate = deposition velocity $*$ pollution concentration,

the ratio of the pollution concentration between years was used to update the flux rate. Arithmetic mean concentration values were used for nitrogen dioxide, particulate matter less than 10 microns, and sulfur dioxide, 2nd Max. 8-hr average for carbon dioxide, and 4th Max. 8-hr average for ozone, to determine

the ratio of change between 1994 and 2000 (U.S. EPA 2003). The new 2000 flux rates were multiplied by urban or community tree cover in the state to estimate total pollution removal by trees.

Pollution removal dollar value estimates were calculated using 1994 national median externality values used in energy decision making (Murray et al. 1994, Ottinger et al. 1990). The 1994 values were adjusted to 2007 dollars based on the producer price index (U.S. Dept. of Labor 2008). These values, in dollars/metric ton (t) are:

- Nitrogen dioxide ($NO_2$) = $9,906/t
- Particulate matter less than 10 microns ($PM_{10}$) = $6,614/t
- Sulfur dioxide ($SO_2$) = $2,425/t
- Carbon monoxide (CO) = $1,407/t

Externality values for ozone ($O_3$) were set to equal the value for $NO_2$. Externality values can be considered the estimated cost of pollution to society that is not accounted for in the market price of the goods or services that produced the pollution.

For each state, Table 1 summarizes carbon storage and air pollution removal estimates for urban, community, and urban or community trees statewide.

## Data Accuracy and Application

The data presented in this report yield the most comprehensive and up-to-date assessment of continental U.S. urban and community forests. The data allows for relative comparisons among geographies and provides baseline information for assessing relative changes in urban and community forest cover in the future. As stated previously, tree cover information was based on finer resolution data than used in the original urban forest assessment (Dwyer et al. 2000). As the methodologies for quantifying tree cover have changed between the original and current assessment, evaluating changes is not possible since the detected changes could be caused by either actual landscape changes or differences in methodology.

The U.S. Census generalized cartographic boundary data are a simplified and smoothed extracts of the Topologically Integrated Geographic Encoding and Referencing (TIGER) database, with a target scale range of 1:5,000,000 (U.S. Census Bureau 2007). Because of this scale and generalization, border simplification impacts attribute measurements that are derived from the boundary data, especially for small areas and at the local scale. In particular, percentages (unitless ratios) generated from attribute measurements made for the smallest communities or county subdivisions may be under- or overstated depending upon the relative location of the smoothed border of the geopolitical unit.

While the 2001 NLCD is a substantial improvement over the 1991 AVHRR data (30-m versus 1-km resolution), it also has local-scale data and application

limitations. Initial tree canopy cover results revealed mean absolute errors (mean of the absolute difference between predicted and actual values) from 8.4 percent to 14.1 percent, with correlation coefficients between predicted and actual values ranging from 0.78 to 0.93. Impervious surface cover results revealed mean absolute errors from 4.6 percent to 7 percent, with $r$-values from 0.83 to 0.91 (Homer et al. 2004).

A more recent analysis of 127 community and 20 county geographies sampled throughout the continental United States compared NLCD tree canopy and impervious surface cover estimates with high resolution (1-m or less resolution) aerial photo-interpreted estimates. This analysis revealed that NLCD underestimates both tree canopy and impervious surface cover compared to photo-interpreted values. NLCD underestimates of tree cover vary by mapping zone, while underestimates of impervious surface cover, which are relatively minor, varies by population density (Greenfield et al. 2009). These findings are consistent with Walton (2008), who found a consistent under-prediction bias for the 2001 NLCD derived tree canopy cover values in census places (communities) of western New York.

The tree cover and impervious cover data given in this report are directly from the NLCD database. To help understand the potential underestimate in the cover values, each U.S. mapping zone was photo-interpreted using Google Earth images[3]. Table B provides a comparison of results from NLCD versus photo-interpreted data for mapping zones applicable to this collection of states.

Comparisons between NLCD impervious surface cover estimates and photo-interpreted values were not reported because differences were related to population density, which can vary significantly among geographic units. Despite the potential underestimates in tree canopy cover values, relative comparisons

---

[3]Nowak, D.J.; Greenfield, E.J. Tree and impervious cover in the conterminous United States: Testing of NLCD cover estimates by mapping zone. In review.

**Table B.—Comparison of NLCD versus photo-interpretation (PI) derived values of percent tree canopy cover by NLCD mapping zones**

| Mapping zone [a] | n [b] | Percent tree canopy cover | | Difference [e] | Margin of error [f] | Significant difference [g] |
|---|---|---|---|---|---|---|
| | | NLCD [c] | PI [d] | | | |
| 29 | 977 | 6.3% | 9.9% | 3.5% | 1.8% | Yes |
| 30 | 771 | 1.1% | 1.8% | 0.8% | 0.9% | No |
| 31 | 624 | 1.9% | 3.8% | 1.9% | 1.4% | Yes |
| 32 | 619 | 13.4% | 23.0% | 9.6% | 2.7% | Yes |
| 33 | 761 | 0.3% | 1.0% | 0.7% | 0.7% | Yes |
| 34 | 929 | 1.2% | 8.1% | 6.9% | 1.7% | Yes |
| 38 | 497 | 3.3% | 4.1% | 0.8% | 1.6% | No |
| 39 | 525 | 0.7% | 2.6% | 2.0% | 1.1% | Yes |
| 40 | 997 | 2.5% | 4.4% | 1.9% | 1.1% | Yes |
| 41 | 885 | 50.1% | 53.2% | 3.0% | 2.6% | Yes |
| 42 | 452 | 7.8% | 10.5% | 2.7% | 2.0% | Yes |
| 43 | 594 | 12.8% | 23.1% | 10.3% | 2.7% | Yes |
| 44 | 913 | 50.0% | 60.6% | 10.7% | 2.1% | Yes |
| 45 | 989 | 17.8% | 23.3% | 5.5% | 1.5% | Yes |
| 47 | 451 | 30.5% | 41.1% | 10.6% | 2.9% | Yes |

[a] NLCD mapping zones
[b] Number of photo-interpreted sample points
[c] Percent tree canopy value derived from NLCD data
[d] Percent tree canopy derived from photo-interpreted data

[e] PI value minus NLCD value
[f] 95% confidence interval of PI value
[g] Significant difference between NLCD and PI values if NLCD value is outside of 95% confidence interval of PI value

of tree cover among geographies in this report (e.g., planting priority index and the ratings of excellent to poor for local government tree cover) are reasonable as the under-prediction of tree cover is fairly consistent within each mapping zone. However, it is important to note that the tree canopy and impervious surface cover could be underestimated, as well as their associated ecosystem services and values. A forthcoming analysis will better assess the accuracy of the NLCD cover maps (Homer et al. 2007), but these maps and data provide comprehensive, consistent, and comparable estimates (with an inherent degree of error and uncertainty) of tree canopy and impervious surface cover to help urban and community forest management, planning and policy making. Higher resolution cover data may provide more accurate results at the local scale, but the NLCD cover maps provide a cost-effective means to consistently assess and compare the relative differences of urban cover types regionally. For more refined and locally appropriate data, local field or high resolution (1 m or less) image analyses are recommended (e.g., i-Tree – www.itreetools.org; UTC – www.nrs.fs.fed.us/urban/utc).

Because of limited urban and community forest field data, data from several urban and community forests were used to estimate the number of trees and carbon storage by trees. These coarse estimates reveal that urban and community forests contain a large number of trees and provide significant environmental benefits. Field data are needed from all states to help improve these estimates as well as to estimate other forest effects (e.g., building energy conservation and changes in stream flow and water quality). Data from long-term monitoring of urban and community forests used in conjunction with satellite-based cover maps will provide essential information to assess forest health and change, and to improve urban and community forest management.

## Practical Applications for Managers

The data from this report can be used to aid urban forest management at both the state and local levels. Data can be used to:

- Determine the extent, magnitude, and variation in the urban and community forestry resource
- Determine areas of greatest population growth, urbanization, and development (sprawl) to direct urban and community forestry to minimize negative impacts and maximize environmental benefits

- Evaluate existing tree canopy, impervious surface cover, and available planting space (available green space) to direct current and future urban and community forestry efforts such as planting programs
- Compare tree canopy cover for similar geopolitical units and set tree canopy goals
- Prioritize tree planting based on population density, tree canopy green space, and tree canopy cover per person
- Understand the pollution removal and carbon storage benefits of urban and community forests
- Promote more detailed and/or locally appropriate urban and community forest inventories, censuses, or field surveys (e.g. i-Tree – www.itreetools.org)
- Establish statewide to local standards related to urban and community forestry (e.g., establishing minimum goals of percent canopy green space or tree cover per capita and directing resources so that communities can reach the minimum standards)
- Improve urban and community forest management and cost estimation by providing an estimate of the number of trees in each geopolitical unit (i.e., urban area size (ha) ∗ percent tree cover ∗ 477 trees/ha, or local tree density information from local data)
- Guide policy decisions related to urban sprawl and urban and community forest management

## SUMMARY

The data presented in this report provide a better understanding of urban and community forests. This information can be used to advance urban and community forest policy and management that could improve environmental quality and human health throughout the state. The following sections detail specific urban and community forestry data for the states in this regional report.

## ACKNOWLEDGMENTS

This research was funded, in part, by the U.S. Forest Service's RPA Assessment Staff, State and Private Forestry's Urban and Community Forestry Program, and Northeastern Area State and Private Forestry. Thanks also goes to Chris Sorrentino for assistance with report compilation, Nana Efua Imbeah for assistance with data processing, and Mike Boarman for assistance with image processing.

# IOWA'S URBAN AND COMMUNITY FORESTS

## Statewide Summary

Urban or community land in Iowa comprises about 3.6 percent of the state land area in 2000, an increase from 3.4 percent in 1990. Statewide tree canopy cover averages 7.8 percent and tree cover in urban or community areas is about 10.4 percent, with 15.1 percent impervious surface cover and 12.2 percent of the total green space covered by tree canopy cover. Statewide, urban or community land in Iowa has an estimated 26 million trees, which store about 5 million metric tons of carbon ($114 million), and annually remove about 163,000 metric tons of carbon ($3.7 million) and 3,520 metric tons of air pollution ($28.0 million) (Table IA-1).

Tables IA-2 through IA-17 are not printed in this report but are available on the CD located on the inside back cover and at http://nrs.fs.fed.us/data/urban.

**Table IA-1.—Statewide summary of population, area, population density, tree canopy and impervious surface land cover, and urban tree benefits in urban, community, and urban or community areas.**

| Iowa | | Statewide | Urban [a] | Community [b] | Urban or Community [c] |
|---|---|---|---|---|---|
| Population | 2000 | 2,926,324 | 1,787,432 | 2,271,662 | n/a |
| | 1990 | 2,776,755 | 1,683,065 | 2,128,172 | n/a |
| | % Change (1990-2000) | 5.4 | 6.2 | 6.7 | n/a |
| | % Total population (2000) | 100.0 | 61.1 | 77.6 | n/a |
| Total area | $km^2$ (2000) | 145,742.6 | 2,120.3 | 5,112.8 | 5,381.0 |
| | $km^2$ (1990) | 145,742.6 | 1,941.8 | 4,767.8 | 5,044.1 |
| | % Change (1990-2000) | 0.0 | 9.2 | 7.2 | 6.7 |
| Land area | $km^2$ (2000) | 144,397.6 | 2,100.7 | 4,994.6 | 5,258.9 |
| | % Land area (2000) | 100.0 | 1.5 | 3.5 | 3.6 |
| | $km^2$ (1990) | 144,397.6 | 1,919.5 | 4,654.8 | 4,926.5 |
| | % Land area (1990) | 100.0 | 1.3 | 3.2 | 3.4 |
| | % Change (1990-2000) | 0.0 | 9.4 | 7.3 | 6.7 |
| Population density (people/land area $km^2$) | 2000 | 20.3 | 850.9 | 454.8 | n/a |
| | 1990 | 19.2 | 876.8 | 457.2 | n/a |
| | % Change (1990-2000) | 5.4 | -3.0 | -0.5 | n/a |
| Tree canopy cover (2000) | $km^2$ | 11,309.3 | 288.1 | 500.4 | 544.9 |
| | % Land area | 7.8 | 13.7 | 10.0 | 10.4 |
| | Per capita ($m^2$/person) | 3,864.7 | 161.2 | 220.3 | n/a |
| | % Canopy green space [d] | 7.9 | 17.9 | 11.9 | 12.2 |
| Total green space (2000) [e] | $km^2$ | 142,757.0 | 1,610.4 | 4,217.7 | 4,466.1 |
| | % Land area | 98.9 | 76.7 | 84.4 | 84.9 |
| Available green space (2000) [f] | $km^2$ | 131,448.0 | 1,322.4 | 3,717.3 | 3,921.2 |
| | % Land area | 91.0 | 63.0 | 74.4 | 74.6 |
| Impervious surface cover (2000) | $km^2$ | 1,640.7 | 490.3 | 776.9 | 792.8 |
| | % Land area | 1.1 | 23.3 | 15.6 | 15.1 |
| | Per capita ($m^2$/person) | 560.7 | 274.3 | 342.0 | n/a |
| Urban tree benefits (2000) | Estimated number of trees | n/a | 13,700,000 | 23,900,000 | 26,000,000 |
| | Carbon | | | | |
| | Carbon stored (metric tons) | n/a | 2,600,000 | 4,600,000 | 5,000,000 |
| | Carbon stored ($) | n/a | $59,300,000 | $104,900,000 | $114,000,000 |
| | Carbon sequestered (metric tons/year) | n/a | 86,000 | 150,000 | 163,000 |
| | Carbon sequestered ($/year) | n/a | $1,961,000 | $3,420,000 | $3,716,000 |
| | Pollution | | | | |
| | CO removed (metric tons/year) | n/a | 34 | 59 | 65 |
| | CO removed ($/year) | n/a | $48,000 | $83,400 | $90,900 |
| | $NO_2$ removed (metric tons/year) | n/a | 421 | 732 | 797 |
| | $NO_2$ removed ($/year) | n/a | $4,171,500 | $7,246,400 | $7,890,500 |
| | $O_3$ removed (metric tons/year) | n/a | 592 | 1,029 | 1,120 |
| | $O_3$ removed ($/year) | n/a | $5,866,000 | $10,190,000 | $11,095,000 |
| | $SO_2$ removed (metric tons/year) | n/a | 159 | 275 | 300 |
| | $SO_2$ removed ($/year) | n/a | $384,500 | $667,900 | $727,300 |
| | $PM_{10}$ removed (metric tons/year) | n/a | 656 | 1,139 | 1,240 |
| | $PM_{10}$ removed ($/year) | n/a | $4,336,700 | $7,533,400 | $8,203,000 |
| | Total pollution removal (metric tons/year) | n/a | 1,860 | 3,230 | 3,520 |
| | Total pollution removal ($/year) | n/a | $14,800,000 | $25,700,000 | $28,000,000 |

[a] Urban land is based on population density and was delimited using the United States Census definitions of urbanized areas and urban clusters.  [b] Community land is based on jurisdictional or political boundaries of communities based on United States Census definitions of incorporated or census designated places. [c] Urban or communities is land that is urban, community, or both. Communities may include all, some, or no urban land within their boundaries.  [d] Canopy green space is the tree canopy cover divided by total green space.  [e] Total green space (TGS) is total area – impervious surface cover – water.  [f] Available green space (AGS) is total green space – tree canopy cover (if the calculated value is less than 0, then value set at 0).

Community Boundaries
Urban Land

Figure IA-1.—Urban or community land
in 2000; urban area relative to community
boundaries.

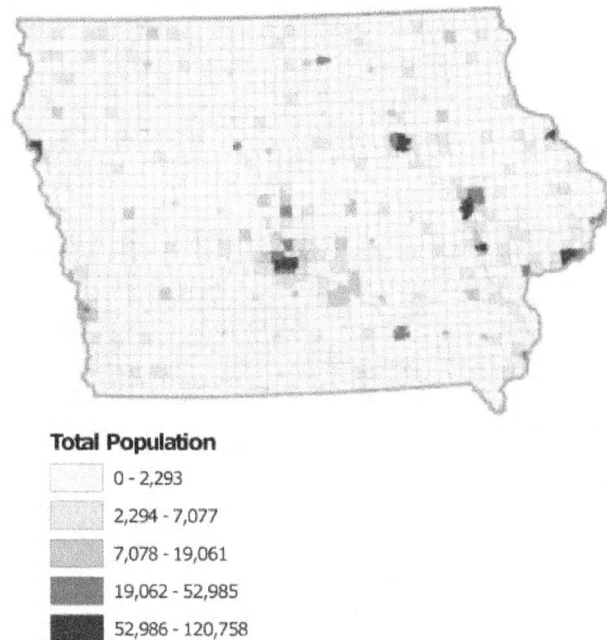

**Total Population**

| | |
|---|---|
| | 0 - 2,293 |
| | 2,294 - 7,077 |
| | 7,078 - 19,061 |
| | 19,062 - 52,985 |
| | 52,986 - 120,758 |

Figure IA-2.—2000 population within
county subdivision boundaries.

## Human Population Characteristics and Trends

The population in Iowa increased 5.4 percent, from
2,776,755 in 1990 to 2,926,324 in 2000 (Table IA-1).
In Iowa, 61.1 percent of the State's population is in
urban areas (Fig. IA-1), and 77.6 percent of the
population is within communities (Fig. IA-2).

## Urban and Community Land

Urban land comprises 1.5 percent of the land area of Iowa,
while lands within communities make up 3.5 percent of
the State (Fig. IA-1). Between 1990 and 2000, urban area
increased 9.4 percent, while community land increased
from 3.2 to 3.5 percent (Table IA-1). Urban area in Iowa
is projected to increase to 4.9 percent by 2050, based
on average urban growth pattern of the 1990s (Nowak
and Walton 2005). Both urban land (attaining minimum
population density) and community land (political
boundaries) increased from 1990 to 2000. The percentages
are calculated using the total (water and land) area of the
geopolitical units derived from U.S. Census cartographic
boundary data. Percent urban land varied across the State
(Fig. IA-3; Tables IA-2 through 4).

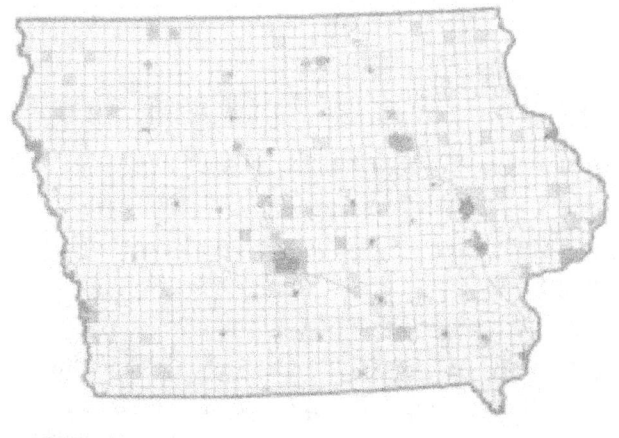

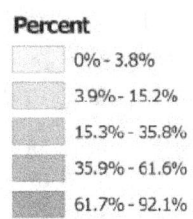

**Percent**

| | |
|---|---|
| | 0% - 3.8% |
| | 3.9% - 15.2% |
| | 15.3% - 35.8% |
| | 35.9% - 61.6% |
| | 61.7% - 92.1% |

Figure IA-3.—Percent of county
subdivision area classified as urban land
in 2000.

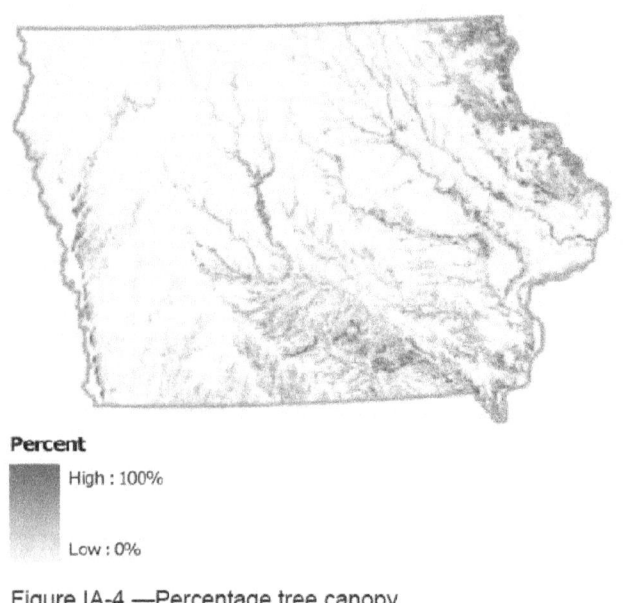

**Percent**

High : 100%

Low : 0%

Figure IA-4.—Percentage tree canopy cover.

**Percent**

0.1% - 4%

4.1% - 10%

10.1% - 18.1%

18.2% - 29.4%

29.5% - 57.9%

Figure IA-5.—Percentage tree canopy cover within county subdivisions.

## Tree Canopy Cover Characteristics

Tree canopy cover in Iowa averages 7.8 percent (Fig. IA-4), with 98.9 percent total green space, 7.9 percent canopy green space, and 3,864.7 m² of canopy cover per capita. Average tree cover in urban areas in Iowa was 13.7 percent, with 76.7 percent total green space, 17.9 percent canopy green space, and 161.2 m² of canopy cover per capita. Within community lands in Iowa, average tree cover was 10.0 percent, with 84.4 percent total green space, 11.9 percent canopy green space, and 220.3 m² of canopy cover per capita (Table IA-1). Tree canopy cover, canopy green space, and tree cover per capita varied among communities, county subdivisions, and counties (Fig. IA-5 through 6; Tables IA-5 through 7).

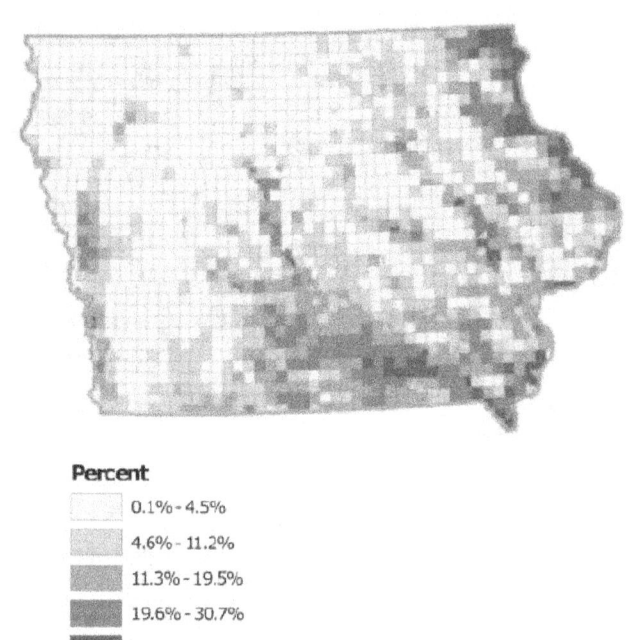

**Percent**

0.1% - 4.5%

4.6% - 11.2%

11.3% - 19.5%

19.6% - 30.7%

30.8% - 58.1%

Figure IA-6.—Percentage tree canopy green space in county subdivisions.

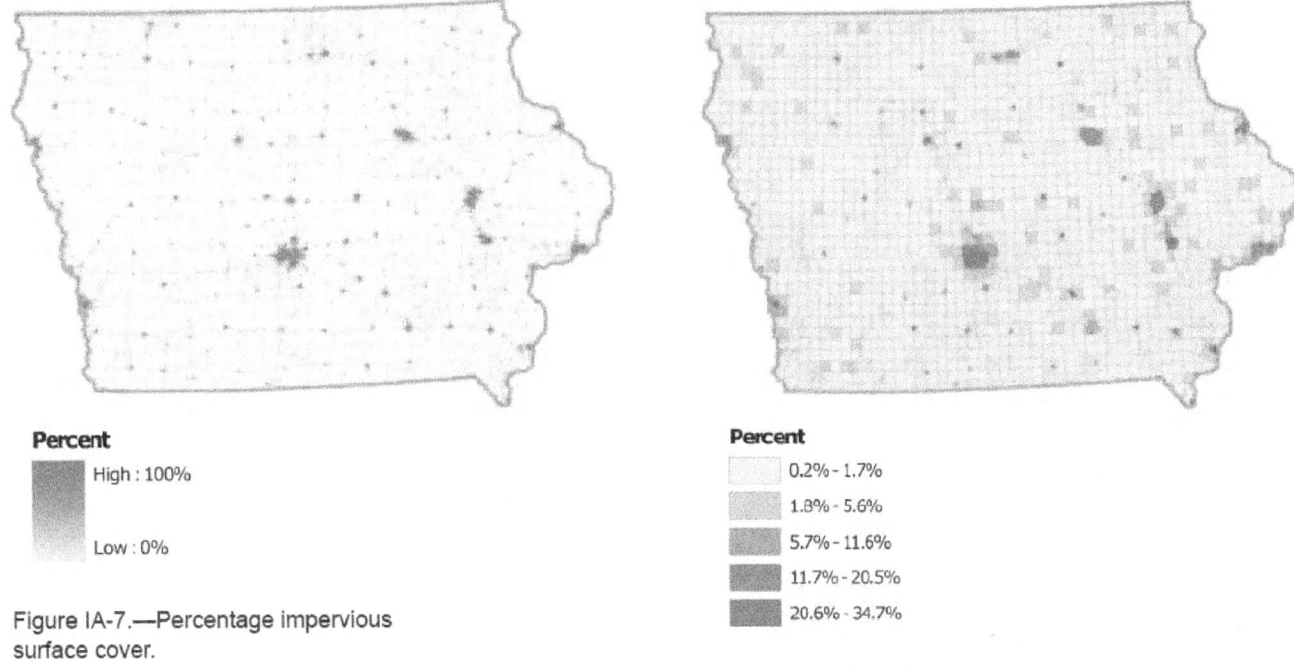

**Percent**

High : 100%

Low : 0%

Figure IA-7.—Percentage impervious surface cover.

**Percent**

0.2% - 1.7%

1.8% - 5.6%

5.7% - 11.6%

11.7% - 20.5%

20.6% - 34.7%

Figure IA-8.—Percentage impervious surface cover within county subdivisions.

## Impervious Surface Cover Characteristics

Average impervious surface cover in Iowa is 1.1 percent of the land area (Fig. IA-7), with 560.7 m$^2$ of impervious surface cover per capita. Average impervious surface cover in urban areas was 23.3 percent, with 274.3 m$^2$ of impervious surface cover per capita. Within community lands in Iowa, average impervious surface cover was 15.6 percent with 342.0 m$^2$ of impervious surface cover per capita (Table IA-1). Impervious surface cover varied across the State (Fig. IA-8; Tables IA-5 through 7).

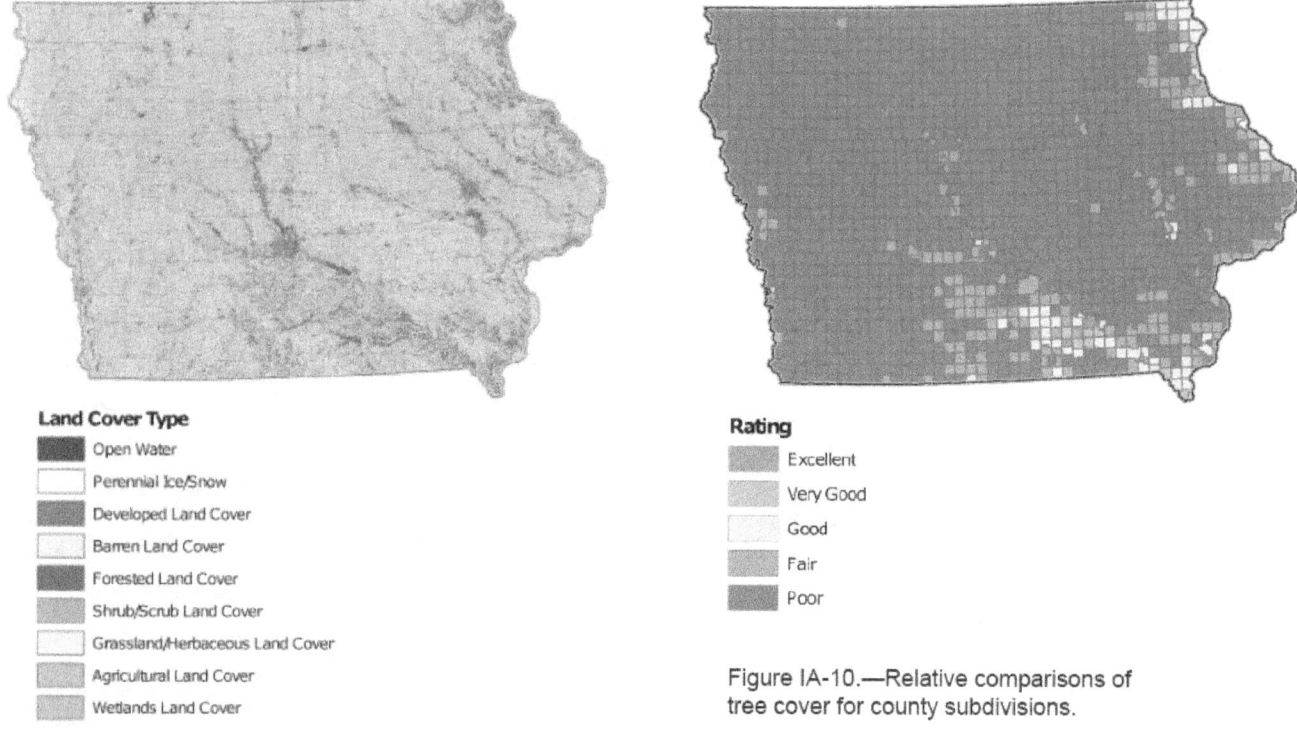

**Land Cover Type**
- Open Water
- Perennial Ice/Snow
- Developed Land Cover
- Barren Land Cover
- Forested Land Cover
- Shrub/Scrub Land Cover
- Grassland/Herbaceous Land Cover
- Agricultural Land Cover
- Wetlands Land Cover

Figure IA-9.—Classified land cover.

**Rating**
- Excellent
- Very Good
- Good
- Fair
- Poor

Figure IA-10.—Relative comparisons of tree cover for county subdivisions.

## Classified Land-cover Characteristics

Iowa's land cover is dominated by agricultural land (Fig. IA-9). The characteristics as a percent of the total land area in Iowa are (Tables IA-8 through 10):

- Agricultural – 80.1 percent
- Developed – 7.4 percent
- Forested – 7.0 percent
- Grassland – 4.8 percent
- Wetland – 0.5 percent
- Scrub/Shrub – 0.2 percent
- Barren – Less than 0.1 percent

## Relative Comparisons of Tree Cover

Out of the 954 Iowa communities, 11 received a rating of excellent and 837 received a rating of poor (Table IA-12). Of the 1,661 county subdivisions, four had a rating of excellent and 1,401 were rated poor (Fig. IA-10, Table IA-13); and out of 99 counties, one was given a rating of excellent and 68 were given a rating of poor (Table IA-14). Variability of assessment scores is a product of the difference in land cover distributions and the percentage of canopy cover within the population density classes and mapping zones (Fig. IA-10; Tables IA-11 through 14).

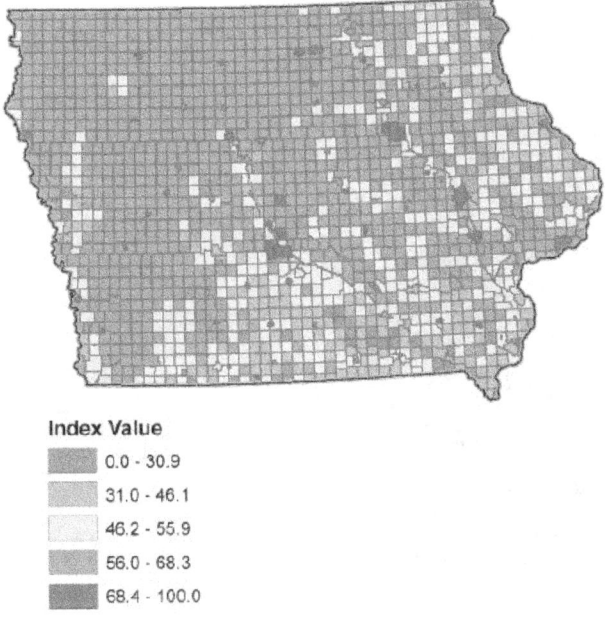

**Index Value**

- 0.0 - 30.9
- 31.0 - 46.1
- 46.2 - 55.9
- 56.0 - 68.3
- 68.4 - 100.0

Figure IA-11.—Planting priority index for county subdivisions. The higher the index value, the greater priority for planting.

## Priority Areas for Tree Planting

Priority areas for planting tend to be highest in more urbanized areas due to higher population density (Fig. IA-11; Tables IA-15 through 17). These index values can also be produced using high resolution cover data to determine local planting priority areas (e.g., neighborhoods).

## Urban Tree Benefits

The following forest attributes are estimated for the urban or community land in Iowa (Table IA-1). These are rough estimates of values. More localized data are needed for more precise estimates, but these values reveal first-order approximations.

- 26 million trees
- 5 million metric tons of C stored ($114 million value)
- 163,000 metric tons/year of C sequestered ($3.7 million value)
- 3,520 metric tons/year total pollution removal ($28.0 million value)
  - 65 metric tons/year of CO removed ($90,900 value)
  - 797 metric tons/year $NO_2$ removed ($7.9 million value)
  - 1,120 metric tons/year of $O_3$ removed ($11.1 million value)
  - 300 metric tons/year of $SO_2$ removed ($727,300 value)
  - 1,240 metric tons/year of $PM_{10}$ removed ($8.2 million value)

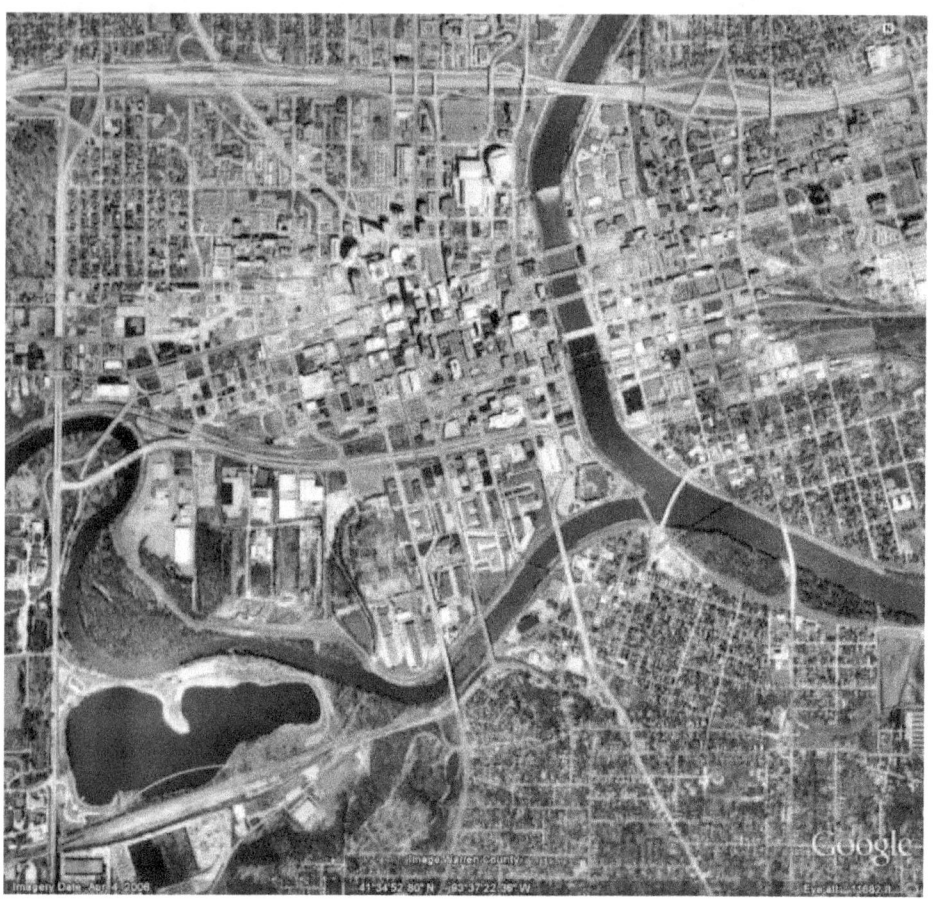

## Summary

The data presented in this report provide a better understanding of Iowa's urban and community forests. This information can be used to advance urban and community forest policy and management that could improve environmental quality and human health throughout the State.

These data establish a baseline to assess future change and can be used to understand:
- Extent of the urban and community forest resource
- Variations in the resource across the State
- Magnitude and value of the urban and community forest resource
- Urban growth in Iowa
- Implications of policy decisions related to urban sprawl and urban and community forest management

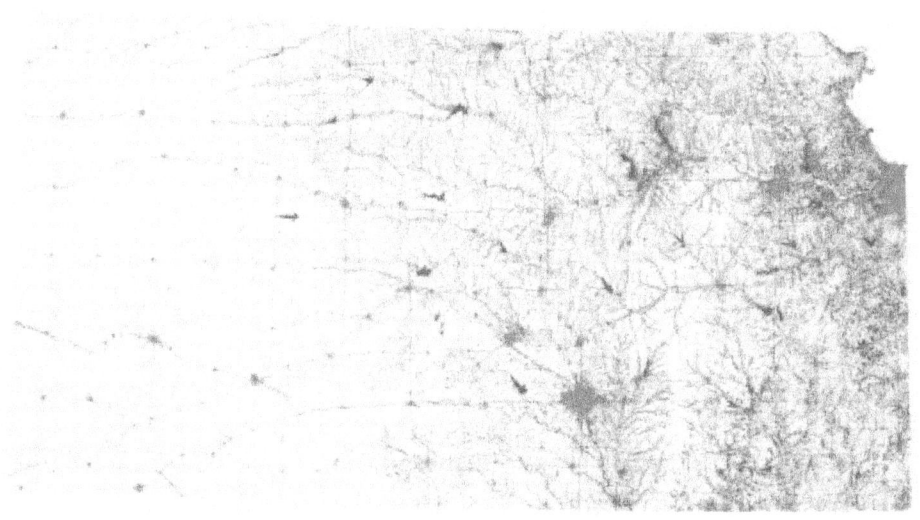

# KANSAS' URBAN
# AND COMMUNITY FORESTS

## Statewide Summary

Urban or community land in Kansas comprises about 1.8 percent of the state land area in 2000, an increase from 1.6 percent in 1990. Statewide tree canopy cover averages 3.6 percent and tree cover in urban or community areas is about 9.1 percent, with 21.6 percent impervious surface cover and 11.6 percent of the total green space covered by tree canopy cover. Statewide, urban or community land in Kansas has an estimated 16.5 million trees, which store about 3.2 million metric tons of carbon ($73.0 million), and annually remove about 104,000 metric tons of carbon ($2.4 million) and 2,690 metric tons of air pollution ($21.3 million) (Table KS-1).

Tables KS-2 through KS-17 are not printed in this report but are available on the CD located on the inside back cover and at http://nrs.fs.fed.us/data/urban.

**Table KS-1.—Statewide summary of population, area, population density, tree canopy and impervious surface land cover, and urban tree benefits in urban, community, and urban or community areas.**

| Kansas | | Statewide | Urban [a] | Community [b] | Urban or Community [c] |
|---|---|---|---|---|---|
| Population | 2000 | 2,688,418 | 1,920,669 | 2,178,835 | n/a |
| | 1990 | 2,477,574 | 1,712,564 | 1,979,241 | n/a |
| | % Change (1990-2000) | 8.5 | 12.2 | 10.1 | n/a |
| | % Total population (2000) | 100.0 | 71.4 | 81.0 | n/a |
| Total area | km² (2000) | 213,096.0 | 2,245.3 | 3,506.2 | 3,893.9 |
| | km² (1990) | 213,096.0 | 1,964.0 | 3,130.8 | 3,478.3 |
| | % Change (1990-2000) | 0.0 | 14.3 | 12.0 | 11.9 |
| Land area | km² (2000) | 210,984.7 | 2,218.1 | 3,438.7 | 3,816.7 |
| | % Land area (2000) | 100.0 | 1.1 | 1.6 | 1.8 |
| | km² (1990) | 210,984.7 | 1,944.4 | 3,077.5 | 3,417.5 |
| | % Land area (1990) | 100.0 | 0.9 | 1.5 | 1.6 |
| | % Change (1990-2000) | 0.0 | 14.1 | 11.7 | 11.7 |
| Population density (people/land area km²) | 2000 | 12.7 | 865.9 | 633.6 | n/a |
| | 1990 | 11.7 | 880.8 | 643.1 | n/a |
| | % Change (1990-2000) | 8.5 | -1.7 | -1.5 | n/a |
| Tree canopy cover (2000) | km² | 7,696.9 | 193.4 | 312.0 | 346.3 |
| | % Land area | 3.6 | 8.7 | 9.1 | 9.1 |
| | Per capita (m²/person) | 2,863.0 | 100.7 | 143.2 | n/a |
| | % Canopy green space [d] | 3.7 | 12.0 | 11.8 | 11.6 |
| Total green space (2000) [e] | km² | 209,314.0 | 1614.2 | 2,648.3 | 2,994.0 |
| | % Land area | 99.2 | 72.8 | 77.0 | 78.4 |
| Available green space (2000) [f] | km² | 201,617.0 | 1,421.0 | 2,336.5 | 2,647.9 |
| | % Land area | 95.6 | 64.1 | 67.9 | 69.4 |
| Impervious surface cover (2000) | km² | 1,671.1 | 604.0 | 790.4 | 822.7 |
| | % Land area | 0.8 | 27.2 | 23.0 | 21.6 |
| | Per capita (m²/person) | 621.6 | 314.5 | 362.8 | n/a |
| Urban tree benefits (2000) | Estimated number of trees | n/a | 9,200,000 | 14,900,000 | 16,500,000 |
| | Carbon | | | | |
| | Carbon stored (metric tons) | n/a | 1,800,000 | 2,800,000 | 3,200,000 |
| | Carbon stored ($) | n/a | $41,000,000 | $63,800,000 | $73,000,000 |
| | Carbon sequestered (metric tons/year) | n/a | 58,000 | 94,000 | 104,000 |
| | Carbon sequestered ($/year) | n/a | $1,322,000 | $2,143,000 | $2,371,000 |
| | Pollution | | | | |
| | CO removed (metric tons/year) | n/a | 30 | 48 | 53 |
| | CO removed ($/year) | n/a | $41,600 | $67,100 | $74,500 |
| | $NO_2$ removed (metric tons/year) | n/a | 142 | 229 | 254 |
| | $NO_2$ removed ($/year) | n/a | $1,406,200 | $2,269,500 | $2,518,600 |
| | $O_3$ removed (metric tons/year) | n/a | 600 | 969 | 1,075 |
| | $O_3$ removed ($/year) | n/a | $5,946,000 | $9,595,000 | $10,649,000 |
| | $SO_2$ removed (metric tons/year) | n/a | 70 | 112 | 125 |
| | $SO_2$ removed ($/year) | n/a | $168,900 | $272,600 | $302,600 |
| | $PM_{10}$ removed (metric tons/year) | n/a | 658 | 1,063 | 1,179 |
| | $PM_{10}$ removed ($/year) | n/a | $4,355,200 | $7,028,600 | $7,800,100 |
| | Total pollution removal (metric tons/year) | n/a | 1,500 | 2,420 | 2,690 |
| | Total pollution removal ($/year) | n/a | $11,900,000 | $19,200,000 | $21,300,000 |

[a] Urban land is based on population density and was delimited using the United States Census definitions of urbanized areas and urban clusters.  [b] Community land is based on jurisdictional or political boundaries of communities based on United States Census definitions of incorporated or census designated places.  [c] Urban or communities is land that is urban, community, or both. Communities may include all, some, or no urban land within their boundaries.  [d] Canopy green space is the tree canopy cover divided by total green space.  [e] Total green space (TGS) is total area – impervious surface cover – water.  [f] Available green space (AGS) is total green space – tree canopy cover (if the calculated value is less than 0, then value set at 0).

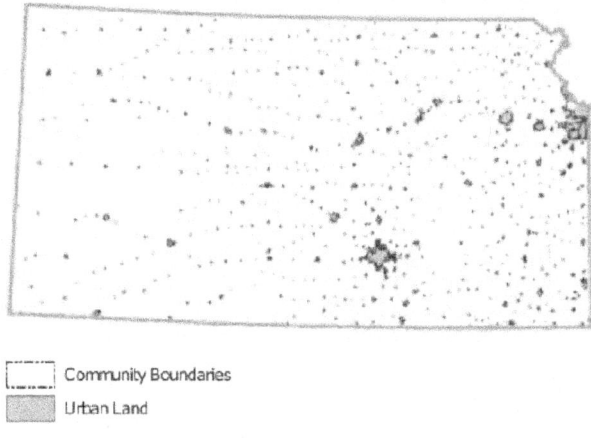

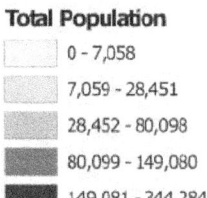

Community Boundaries

Urban Land

Figure KS-1.—Urban or community land in 2000; urban area relative to community boundaries.

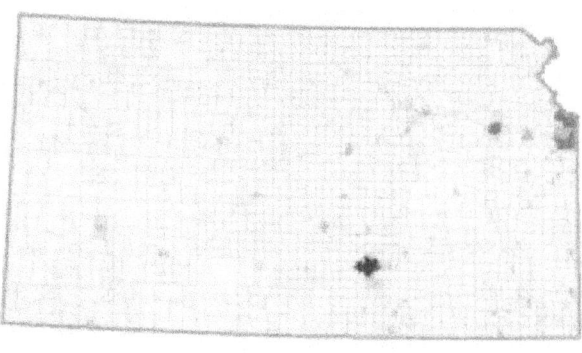

**Total Population**

0 - 7,058

7,059 - 28,451

28,452 - 80,098

80,099 - 149,080

149,081 - 344,284

Figure KS-2.—2000 population within county subdivision boundaries.

## Human Population Characteristics and Trends

The population in Kansas increased 8.5 percent, from 2,477,574 in 1990 to 2,688,418 in 2000 (Table KS-1). In Kansas, 71.4 percent of the State's population is in urban areas (Fig. KS-1), and 81.0 percent of the population is within communities (Fig. KS-2).

## Urban and Community Land

Urban land comprises 1.1 percent of the land area of Kansas, while lands within communities make up 1.6 percent of the State (Fig. KS-1). Between 1990 and 2000, urban area increased 14.1 percent, while community land increased from 1.5 to 1.6 percent (Table KS-1). Urban area in Kansas is projected to increase to 3.2 percent by 2050, based on average urban growth pattern of the 1990s (Nowak and Walton 2005). Both urban land (attaining minimum population density) and community land (political boundaries) increased from 1990 to 2000. The percentages are calculated using the total (water and land) area of the geopolitical units derived from U.S. Census cartographic boundary data. Percent urban land varied across the State (Fig. KS-3; Tables KS-2 through 4).

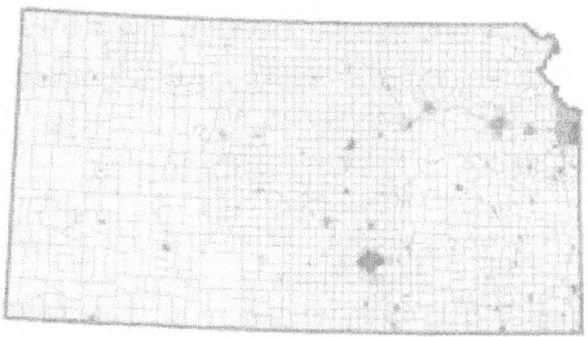

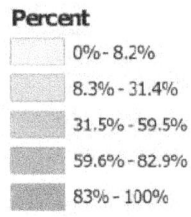

**Percent**

0% - 8.2%

8.3% - 31.4%

31.5% - 59.5%

59.6% - 82.9%

83% - 100%

Figure KS-3.—Percent of county subdivision area classified as urban land in 2000.

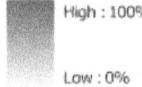

**Percent**

High : 100%

Low : 0%

Figure KS-4.——Percentage tree canopy cover.

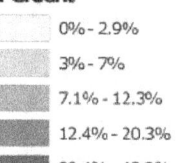

**Percent**

0% - 2.9%

3% - 7%

7.1% - 12.3%

12.4% - 20.3%

20.4% - 42.2%

Figure KS-5.——Percentage tree canopy cover within county subdivisions.

## Tree Canopy Cover Characteristics

Tree canopy cover in Kansas averages 3.6 percent (Fig. KS-4), with 99.2 percent total green space, 3.7 percent canopy green space, and 2,863.0 m$^2$ of canopy cover per capita. Average tree cover in urban areas in Kansas was 8.7 percent, with 72.8 percent total green space, 12.0 percent canopy green space, and 100.7 m$^2$ of canopy cover per capita. Within community lands in Kansas, average tree cover was 9.1 percent, with 77.0 percent total green space, 11.8 percent canopy green space, and 143.2 m$^2$ of canopy cover per capita (Table KS-1). Tree canopy cover, canopy green space, and tree cover per capita varied among communities, county subdivisions, and counties (Fig. KS-5 through 6; Tables KS-5 through 7).

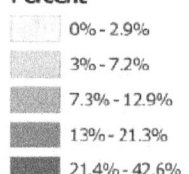

**Percent**

0% - 2.9%

3% - 7.2%

7.3% - 12.9%

13% - 21.3%

21.4% - 42.6%

Figure KS-6.——Percentage tree canopy green space in county subdivisions.

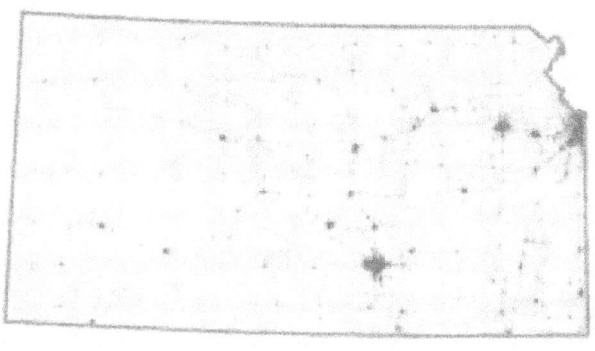

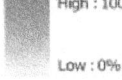
Figure KS-7.—Percentage impervious surface cover.

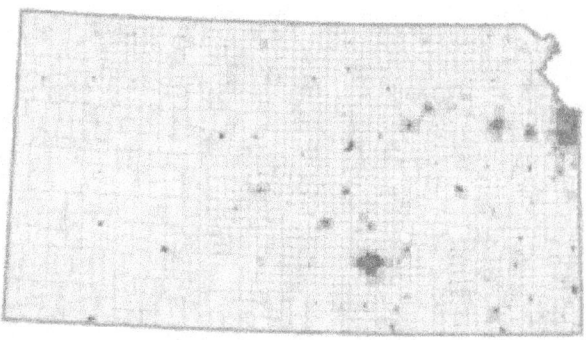

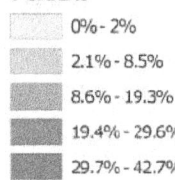
Figure KS-8.—Percentage impervious surface cover within county subdivisions.

## Impervious Surface Cover Characteristics

Average impervious surface cover in Kansas is 0.8 percent of the land area (Fig. KS-7), with 621.6 $m^2$ of impervious surface cover per capita. Average impervious surface cover in urban areas was 27.2 percent, with 314.5 $m^2$ of impervious surface cover per capita. Within community lands in Kansas, average impervious surface cover was 23.0 percent with 362.8 $m^2$ of impervious surface cover per capita (Table KS-1). Impervious surface cover varied across the State (Fig. KS-8; Tables KS-5 through 7).

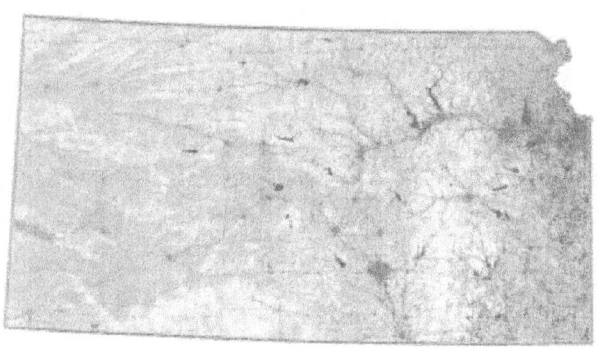

**Land Cover Type**
- Open Water
- Perennial Ice/Snow
- Developed Land Cover
- Barren Land Cover
- Forested Land Cover
- Shrub/Scrub Land Cover
- Grassland/Herbaceous Land Cover
- Agricultural Land Cover
- Wetlands Land Cover

**Rating**
- Excellent
- Very Good
- Good
- Fair
- Poor

Figure KS-10.—Relative comparisons of tree cover for county subdivisions.

Figure KS-9.—Classified land cover.

## Classified Land-cover Characteristics

Kansas land cover is dominated by agricultural land (Fig. KS-9). The characteristics as a percent of the total land area in Kansas are (Tables KS-8 through 10):

- Agricultural – 53.5 percent
- Grassland – 37.1 percent
- Developed – 5.1 percent
- Forested – 3.8 percent
- Scrub/Shrub – 0.4 percent
- Wetland – 0.1 percent
- Barren – 0.1 percent

## Relative Comparisons of Tree Cover

Out of the 631 Kansas communities, nine received a rating of excellent and 518 received a rating of poor (Table KS-12). Of the 1,535 county subdivisions, three had a rating of excellent and 1,422 were rated poor (Fig. KS-10, Table KS-13); and out of 105 counties, two were given a rating of excellent and 76 were given a rating of poor (Table KS-14). Variability of assessment scores is a product of the difference in land cover distributions and the percentage of canopy cover within the population density classes and mapping zones (Fig. KS-10; Tables KS-11 through 14).

**Index Value**

- 0.0 - 26.2
- 26.3 - 37.6
- 37.7 - 44.3
- 44.4 - 55.9
- 56.0 - 100.0

Figure KS-11.—Planting priority index for county subdivisions. The higher the index value, the greater priority for planting.

## Priority Areas for Tree Planting

Priority areas for planting tend to be highest in more urbanized areas due to higher population density (Fig. KS-11; Tables KS-15 through 17). These index values can also be produced using high resolution cover data to determine local planting priority areas (e.g., neighborhoods).

## Urban Tree Benefits

The following forest attributes are estimated for the urban or community land in Kansas (Table KS-1). These are rough estimates of values. More localized data are needed for more precise estimates, but these values reveal first-order approximations.

- 16.5 million trees
- 3.2 million metric tons of C stored ($73.0 million value)
- 104,000 metric tons/year of C sequestered ($2.4 million value)
- 2,690 metric tons/year total pollution removal ($21.3 million value)
  - 53 metric tons/year of CO removed ($74,500 value)
  - 254 metric tons/year $NO_2$ removed ($2.5 million value)
  - 1,075 metric tons/year of $O_3$ removed ($10.6 million value)
  - 125 metric tons/year of $SO_2$ removed ($302,600 value)
  - 1,179 metric tons/year of $PM_{10}$ removed ($7.8 million value).

## Summary

The data presented in this report provide a better understanding of Kansas' urban and community forests. This information can be used to advance urban and community forest policy and management that could improve environmental quality and human health throughout the State.

These data establish a baseline to assess future change and can be used to understand:
- Extent of the urban and community forest resource
- Variations in the resource across the State
- Magnitude and value of the urban and community forest resource
- Urban growth in Kansas
- Implications of policy decisions related to urban sprawl and urban and community forest management

# MINNESOTA'S URBAN AND COMMUNITY FORESTS

## Statewide Summary

Urban or community land in Minnesota comprises about 5.2 percent of the state land area in 2000, an increase from 4.7 percent in 1990. Statewide tree canopy cover averages 30.9 percent and tree cover in urban or community areas is about 27.1 percent, with 12.3 percent impervious surface cover and 30.9 percent of the total green space covered by tree canopy cover. Statewide, urban or community land in Minnesota has an estimated 137 million trees, which store about 26.1 million metric tons of carbon ($595.1 million), and annually remove about 862,000 metric tons of carbon ($19.7 million) and 15,760 metric tons of air pollution ($138.2 million) (Table MN-1).

Tables MN-2 through MN-17 are not printed in this report but are available on the CD located on the inside back cover and at http://nrs.fs.fed.us/data/urban.

**Table MN-1.—Statewide summary of population, area, population density, tree canopy and impervious surface land cover, and urban tree benefits in urban, community, and urban or community areas.**

| Minnesota | | Statewide | Urban [a] | Community [b] | Urban or Community [c] |
|---|---|---|---|---|---|
| Population | 2000 | 4,919,479 | 3,490,059 | 3,939,152 | n/a |
| | 1990 | 4,375,099 | 3,056,474 | 3,387,134 | n/a |
| | % Change (1990-2000) | 12.4 | 14.2 | 16.3 | n/a |
| | % Total population (2000) | 100.0 | 70.9 | 80.1 | n/a |
| Total area | km$^2$ (2000) | 225.170.6 | 4,101.1 | 11,018.2 | 11,409.9 |
| | km$^2$ (1990) | 225.170.6 | 3,532.1 | 9,964.3 | 10,364.4 |
| | % Change (1990-2000) | 0.0 | 16.1 | 10.6 | 10.1 |
| Land area | km$^2$ (2000) | 205,850.8 | 3,877.9 | 10,247.9 | 10,604.4 |
| | % Land area (2000) | 100.0 | 1.9 | 5.0 | 5.2 |
| | km$^2$ (1990) | 205,850.8 | 3,339.2 | 9,293.8 | 9,657.8 |
| | % Land area (1990) | 100.0 | 1.6 | 4.5 | 4.7 |
| | % Change (1990-2000) | 0.0 | 16.1 | 10.3 | 9.8 |
| Population density (people/land area km$^2$) | 2000 | 23.9 | 900.0 | 384.4 | n/a |
| | 1990 | 21.3 | 915.3 | 364.5 | n/a |
| | % Change (1990-2000) | 12.4 | -1.7 | 5.5 | n/a |
| Tree canopy cover (2000) | km$^2$ | 63,612.3 | 715.4 | 2,805.8 | 2,873.1 |
| | % Land area | 30.9 | 18.4 | 27.4 | 27.1 |
| | Per capita (m$^2$/person) | 12,930.7 | 205.0 | 712.3 | n/a |
| | % Canopy green space [d] | 31.2 | 24.8 | 31.3 | 30.9 |
| Total green space (2000) [e] | km$^2$ | 203,705.0 | 2,886.6 | 8,977.0 | 9,305.2 |
| | % Land area | 99.0 | 74.4 | 87.6 | 87.7 |
| Available green space (2000) [f] | km$^2$ | 140,097.0 | 2,172.5 | 6,172.7 | 6,433.7 |
| | % Land area | 68.1 | 56.0 | 60.2 | 60.7 |
| Impervious surface cover (2000) | km$^2$ | 2,146.2 | 991.3 | 1,270.9 | 1,299.1 |
| | % Land area | 1.0 | 25.6 | 12.4 | 12.3 |
| | Per capita (m$^2$/person) | 436.3 | 284.0 | 322.6 | n/a |
| Urban tree benefits (2000) | Estimated number of trees | n/a | 34,100,000 | 133,800,000 | 137,000,000 |
| | Carbon | | | | |
| | Carbon stored (metric tons) | n/a | 6,500,000 | 25,500,000 | 26,100,000 |
| | Carbon stored ($) | n/a | $148,200,000 | $581,400,000 | $595,100,000 |
| | Carbon sequestered (metric tons/year) | n/a | 215,000 | 842,000 | 862,000 |
| | Carbon sequestered ($/year) | n/a | $4,902,000 | $19,198,000 | $19,654,000 |
| | Pollution | | | | |
| | CO removed (metric tons/year) | n/a | 125 | 488 | 500 |
| | CO removed ($/year) | n/a | $175,200 | $687,100 | $703,600 |
| | NO$_2$ removed (metric tons/year) | n/a | 885 | 3,472 | 3,555 |
| | NO$_2$ removed ($/year) | n/a | $8,769,100 | $34,393,900 | $35,218,800 |
| | O$_3$ removed (metric tons/year) | n/a | 2,032 | 7,968 | 8,160 |
| | O$_3$ removed ($/year) | n/a | $20,125,000 | $78,935,000 | $80,829,000 |
| | SO$_2$ removed (metric tons/year) | n/a | 121 | 474 | 486 |
| | SO$_2$ removed ($/year) | n/a | $293,200 | $1,150,100 | $1,177,700 |
| | PM$_{10}$ removed (metric tons/year) | n/a | 763 | 2,991 | 3,063 |
| | PM$_{10}$ removed ($/year) | n/a | $5,044,500 | $19,785,300 | $20,259,800 |
| | Total pollution removal (metric tons/year) | n/a | 3,930 | 15,390 | 15,760 |
| | Total pollution removal ($/year) | n/a | $34,400,000 | $135,000,000 | $138,200,000 |

[a] Urban land is based on population density and was delimited using the United States Census definitions of urbanized areas and urban clusters.  [b] Community land is based on jurisdictional or political boundaries of communities based on United States Census definitions of incorporated or census designated places.  [c] Urban or communities is land that is urban, community, or both. Communities may include all, some, or no urban land within their boundaries.  [d] Canopy green space is the tree canopy cover divided by total green space.  [e] Total green space (TGS) is total area – impervious surface cover – water.  [f] Available green space (AGS) is total green space – tree canopy cover (if the calculated value is less than 0, then value set at 0).

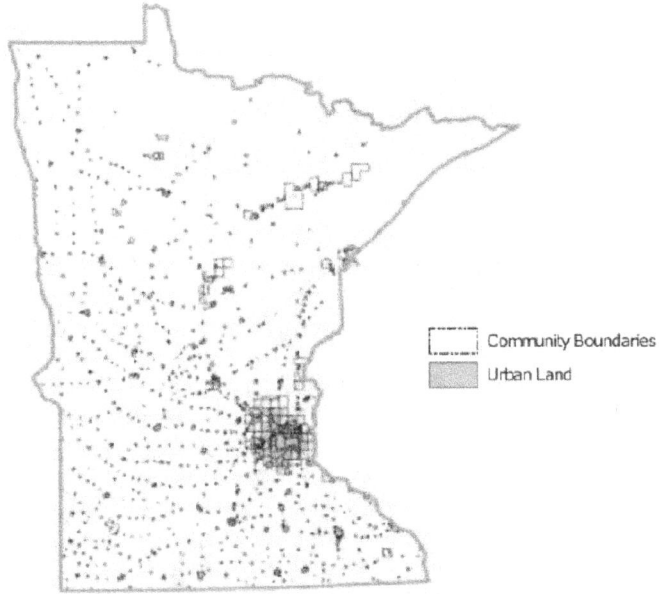

Figure MN-1.—Urban or community land in 2000; urban area relative to community boundaries.

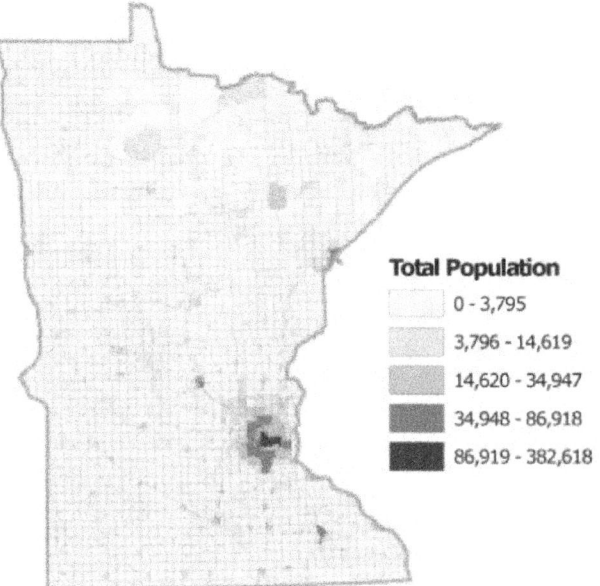

Figure MN-2.—2000 population within county subdivision boundaries.

## Human Population Characteristics and Trends

The population in Minnesota increased 12.4 percent, from 4,375,099 in 1990 to 4,919,479 in 2000 (Table MN-1). In Minnesota, 70.9 percent of the State's population is in urban areas (Fig. MN-1), and 80.1 percent of the population is within communities (Fig. MN-2).

## Urban and Community Land

Urban land comprises 1.9 percent of the land area of Minnesota, while lands within communities make up 5.0 percent of the State (Fig. MN-1). Between 1990 and 2000, urban area increased 16.1 percent, while community land increased from 4.5 to 5.0 percent (Table MN-1). Urban area in Minnesota is projected to increase to 4.8 percent by 2050, based on average urban growth pattern of the 1990s (Nowak and Walton 2005). Both urban land (attaining minimum population density) and community land (political boundaries) increased from 1990 to 2000. The percentages are calculated using the total (water and land) area of the geopolitical units derived from U.S. Census cartographic boundary data. Percent urban land varied across the State (Fig. MN-3; Tables MN-2 through 4).

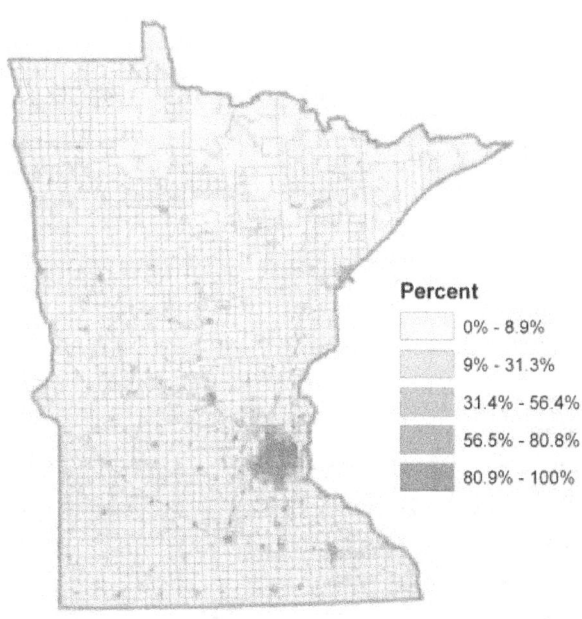

Figure MN-3.—Percent of county subdivision area classified as urban land in 2000.

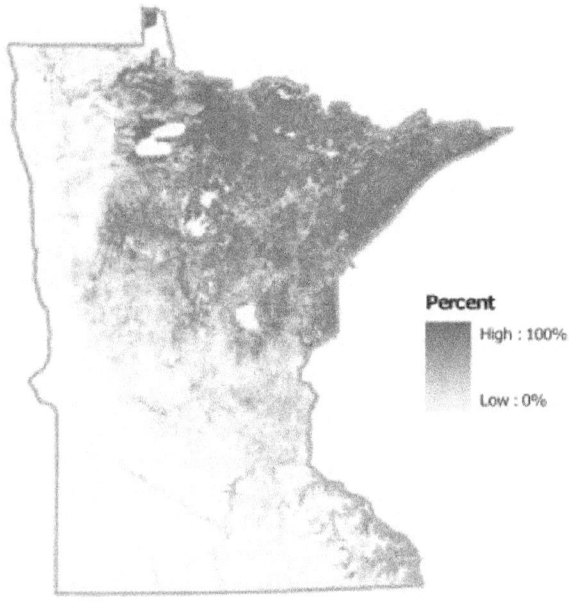

Figure MN-4.—Percentage tree canopy cover.

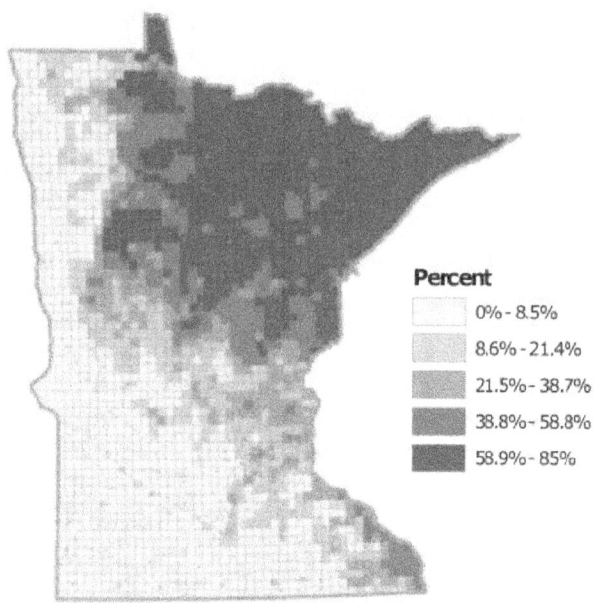

Percent

- 0% - 8.5%
- 8.6% - 21.4%
- 21.5% - 38.7%
- 38.8% - 58.8%
- 58.9% - 85%

Figure MN-5.—Percentage tree canopy cover within county subdivisions.

## Tree Canopy Cover Characteristics

Tree canopy cover in Minnesota averages 30.9 percent (Fig. MN-4), with 99.0 percent total green space, 31.2 percent canopy green space, and 12,930.7 m$^2$ of canopy cover per capita. Average tree cover in urban areas in Minnesota was 18.4 percent, with 74.4 percent total green space, 24.8 percent canopy green space, and 205.0 m$^2$ of canopy cover per capita. Within community lands in Minnesota, average tree cover was 27.4 percent, with 87.6 percent total green space, 31.3 percent canopy green space, and 712.3 m$^2$ of canopy cover per capita (Table MN-1). Tree canopy cover, canopy green space, and tree cover per capita varied among communities, county subdivisions, and counties (Fig. MN-5 through 6; Tables MN-5 through 7).

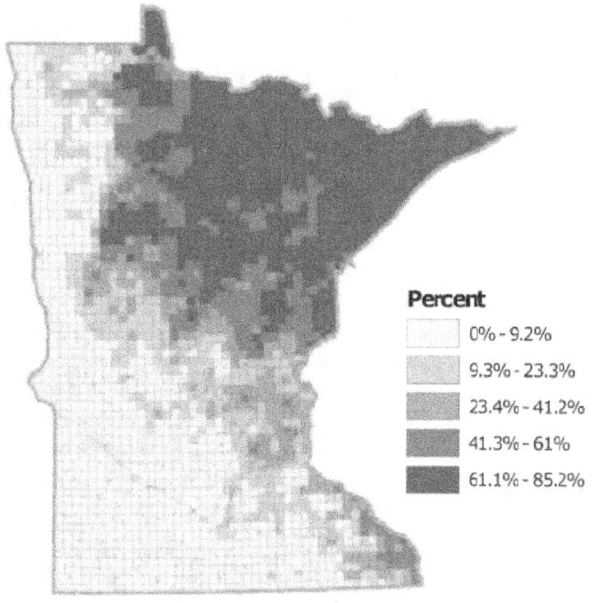

Percent

- 0% - 9.2%
- 9.3% - 23.3%
- 23.4% - 41.2%
- 41.3% - 61%
- 61.1% - 85.2%

Figure MN-6.—Percentage tree canopy green space in county subdivisions.

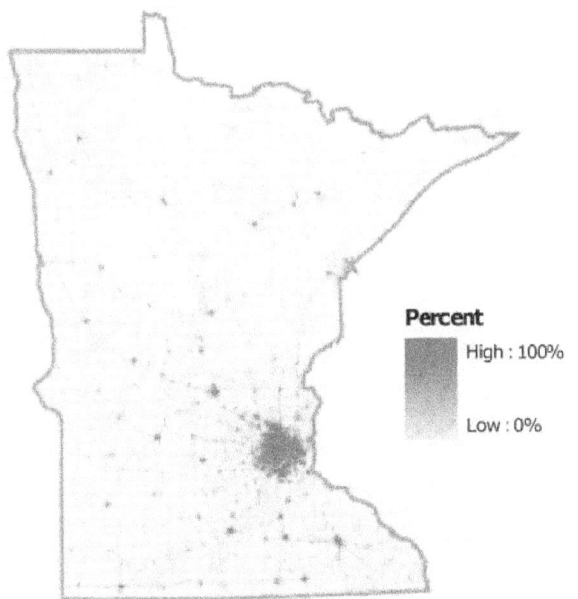

Figure MN-7.—Percentage impervious surface cover.

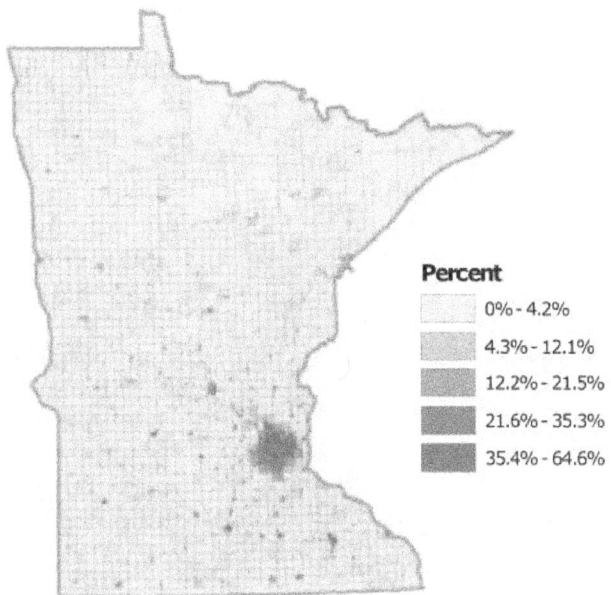

Figure MN-8.—Percentage impervious surface cover within county subdivisions.

## Impervious Surface Cover Characteristics

Average impervious surface cover in Minnesota is 1.0 percent of the land area (Fig. MN-7), with 436.3 $m^2$ of impervious surface cover per capita. Average impervious surface cover in urban areas was 25.6 percent, with 284.0 $m^2$ of impervious surface cover per capita. Within community lands in Minnesota, average impervious surface cover was 12.4 percent with 322.6 $m^2$ of impervious surface cover per capita (Table MN-1). Impervious surface cover varied across the State (Fig. MN-8; Tables MN-5 through 7).

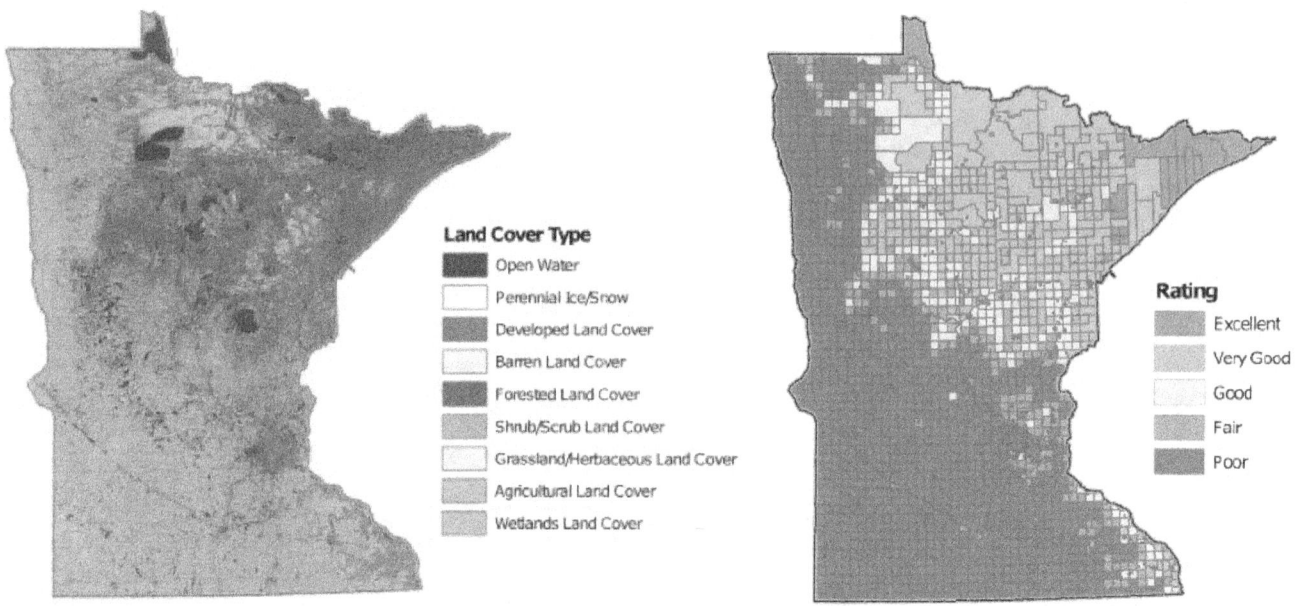

Figure MN-9.—Classified land cover.

Figure MN-10.—Relative comparisons of tree cover for county subdivisions.

## Classified Land-cover Characteristics

Minnesota's land cover is dominated by agricultural land (Fig. MN-9). The characteristics as a percent of the total land area in Minnesota are (Tables MN-8 through 10):

- Agricultural – 54.2 percent
- Forested – 29.0 percent
- Wetland – 6.9 percent
- Developed – 5.4 percent
- Grassland – 2.9 percent
- Scrub/Shrub – 1.4 percent
- Barren – 0.1 percent

## Relative Comparisons of Tree Cover

Out of the 867 Minnesota communities, 22 received a rating of excellent and 583 received a rating of poor (Table MN-12). Of the 2,775 county subdivisions, 45 had a rating of excellent and 1,795 were rated poor (Fig. MN-10, Table MN-13); and out of 87 counties, eight were given a rating of excellent and 44 were given a rating of poor (Table MN-14). Variability of assessment scores is a product of the difference in land cover distributions and the percentage of canopy cover within the population density classes and mapping zones (Fig. MN-10; Tables MN-11 through 14).

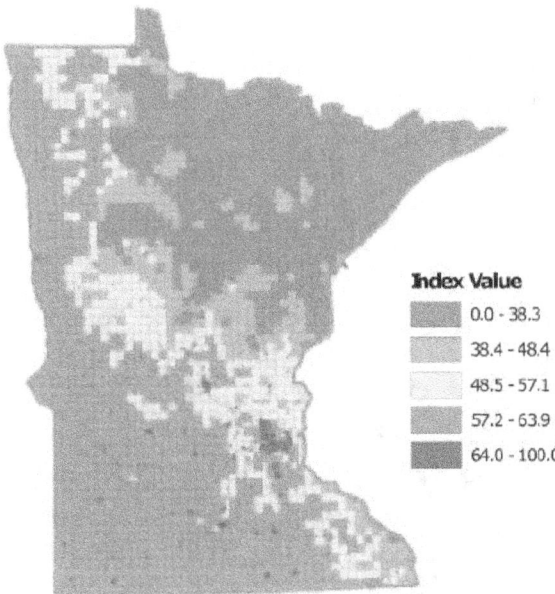

**Index Value**

- 0.0 - 38.3
- 38.4 - 48.4
- 48.5 - 57.1
- 57.2 - 63.9
- 64.0 - 100.0

Figure MN-11.—Planting priority index for county subdivisions. The higher the index value, the greater priority for planting.

## Priority Areas for Tree Planting

Priority areas for planting tend to be highest in more urbanized areas due to higher population density (Fig. MN-11; Tables MN-15 through 17). These index values can also be produced using high resolution cover data to determine local planting priority areas (e.g., neighborhoods).

## Urban Tree Benefits

The following forest attributes are estimated for the urban or community land in Minnesota (Table MN-1). These are rough estimates of values. More localized data are needed for more precise estimates, but these values reveal first-order approximations.

- 137 million trees
- 26.1 million metric tons of C stored ($595.1 million value)
- 862,000 metric tons/year of C sequestered ($19.7 million value)
- 15,760 metric tons/year total pollution removal ($138.2 million value)
  - 500 metric tons/year of CO removed ($703,600 value)
  - 3,555 metric tons/year $NO_2$ removed ($35.2 million value)
  - 8,160 metric tons/year of $O_3$ removed ($80.8 million value)
  - 486 metric tons/year of $SO_2$ removed ($1.2 million value)
  - 3,063 metric tons/year of $PM_{10}$ removed ($20.3 million value)

## Summary

The data presented in this report provide a better understanding of Minnesota's urban and community forests. This information can be used to advance urban and community forest policy and management that could improve environmental quality and human health throughout the State.

These data establish a baseline to assess future change and can be used to understand:

- Extent of the urban and community forest resource
- Variations in the resource across the State
- Magnitude and value of the urban and community forest resource
- Urban growth in Minnesota
- Implications of policy decisions related to urban sprawl and urban and community forest management

## MISSOURI'S URBAN
## AND COMMUNITY FORESTS

### Statewide Summary

Urban or community land in Missouri comprises about 4.7 percent of the state land area in 2000, an increase from 4.1 percent in 1990. Statewide tree canopy cover averages 32.3 percent and tree cover in urban or community areas is about 22.7 percent, with 17.6 percent impervious surface cover and 27.5 percent of the total green space covered by tree canopy cover. Statewide, urban or community land in Missouri has an estimated 90.3 million trees, which store about 17.2 million metric tons of carbon ($392.2 million), and annually remove about 568,000 metric tons of carbon ($13.0 million) and 15,390 metric tons of air pollution ($125.0 million) (Table MO-1).

Tables MO-2 through MO-17 are not printed in this report but are available on the CD located on the inside back cover and at http://nrs.fs.fed.us/data/urban.

**Table MO-1.—Statewide summary of population, area, population density, tree canopy and impervious surface land cover, and urban tree benefits in urban, community, and urban or community areas.**

| Missouri | | Statewide | Urban [a] | Community [b] | Urban or Community [c] |
|---|---|---|---|---|---|
| Population | 2000 | 5,595,211 | 3,883,442 | 3,861,559 | n/a |
| | 1990 | 5,117,073 | 3,516,009 | 3,553,914 | n/a |
| | % Change (1990-2000) | 9.3 | 10.5 | 8.7 | n/a |
| | % Total population (2000) | 100.0 | 69.4 | 69.0 | n/a |
| Total area | km$^2$ (2000) | 180,553.3 | 4,727.3 | 7,598.9 | 8,509.4 |
| | km$^2$ (1990) | 180,553.3 | 4,190.8 | 6,537.9 | 7,388.6 |
| | % Change (1990-2000) | 0.0 | 12.8 | 16.2 | 15.2 |
| Land area | km$^2$ (2000) | 177,995.5 | 4,694.9 | 7,442.1 | 8,345.1 |
| | % Land area (2000) | 100.0 | 2.6 | 4.2 | 4.7 |
| | km$^2$ (1990) | 177,995.5 | 4,163.8 | 6,423.4 | 7,267.4 |
| | % Land area (1990) | 100.0 | 2.3 | 3.6 | 4.1 |
| | % Change (1990-2000) | 0.0 | 12.8 | 15.9 | 14.8 |
| Population density (people/land area km$^2$) | 2000 | 31.4 | 827.2 | 518.9 | n/a |
| | 1990 | 28.7 | 844.4 | 553.3 | n/a |
| | % Change (1990-2000) | 9.3 | -2.0 | -6.2 | n/a |
| Tree canopy cover (2000) | km$^2$ | 57,547.9 | 966.4 | 1,640.6 | 1,893.1 |
| | % Land area | 32.3 | 20.6 | 22.0 | 22.7 |
| | Per capita (m$^2$/person) | 10,285.2 | 248.8 | 424.9 | n/a |
| | % Canopy green space [d] | 32.8 | 27.4 | 27.0 | 27.5 |
| Total green space (2000) [e] | km$^2$ | 175,605.0 | 3,527.5 | 6,085.3 | 6,877.3 |
| | % Land area | 98.7 | 75.1 | 81.8 | 82.4 |
| Available green space (2000) [f] | km$^2$ | 118,063.0 | 2,565.2 | 4,448.4 | 4,988.3 |
| | % Land area | 66.3 | 54.6 | 59.8 | 59.8 |
| Impervious surface cover (2000) | km$^2$ | 2,390.3 | 1,167.4 | 1,356.8 | 1,467.8 |
| | % Land area | 1.3 | 24.9 | 18.2 | 17.6 |
| | Per capita (m$^2$/person) | 427.2 | 300.6 | 351.4 | n/a |
| Urban tree benefits (2000) | Estimated number of trees | n/a | 46,100,000 | 78,200,000 | 90,300,000 |
| | **Carbon** | | | | |
| | Carbon stored (metric tons) | n/a | 8,800,000 | 14,900,000 | 17,200,000 |
| | Carbon stored ($) | n/a | $200,600,000 | $339,700,000 | $392,200,000 |
| | Carbon sequestered (metric tons/year) | n/a | 290,000 | 492,000 | 568,000 |
| | Carbon sequestered ($/year) | n/a | $6,612,000 | $11,218,000 | $12,950,000 |
| | **Pollution** | | | | |
| | CO removed (metric tons/year) | n/a | 132 | 224 | 258 |
| | CO removed ($/year) | n/a | $185,600 | $315,000 | $363,500 |
| | NO$_2$ removed (metric tons/year) | n/a | 1,025 | 1,740 | 2,008 |
| | NO$_2$ removed ($/year) | n/a | $10,152,300 | $17,235,700 | $19,888,600 |
| | O$_3$ removed (metric tons/year) | n/a | 3,584 | 6,085 | 7,022 |
| | O$_3$ removed ($/year) | n/a | $35,506,000 | $60,278,000 | $69,556,000 |
| | SO$_2$ removed (metric tons/year) | n/a | 634 | 1,076 | 1,242 |
| | SO$_2$ removed ($/year) | n/a | $1,537,100 | $2,609,500 | $3,011,100 |
| | PM$_{10}$ removed (metric tons/year) | n/a | 2,483 | 4,215 | 4,863 |
| | PM$_{10}$ removed ($/year) | n/a | $16,419,600 | $27,875,700 | $32,166,300 |
| | Total pollution removal (metric tons/year) | n/a | 7,860 | 13,340 | 15,390 |
| | Total pollution removal ($/year) | n/a | $63,800,000 | $108,300,000 | $125,000,000 |

[a] Urban land is based on population density and was delimited using the United States Census definitions of urbanized areas and urban clusters. [b] Community land is based on jurisdictional or political boundaries of communities based on United States Census definitions of incorporated or census designated places. [c] Urban or communities is land that is urban, community, or both. Communities may include all, some, or no urban land within their boundaries. [d] Canopy green space is the tree canopy cover divided by total green space. [e] Total green space (TGS) is total area – impervious surface cover – water. [f] Available green space (AGS) is total green space – tree canopy cover (if the calculated value is less than 0, then value set at 0).

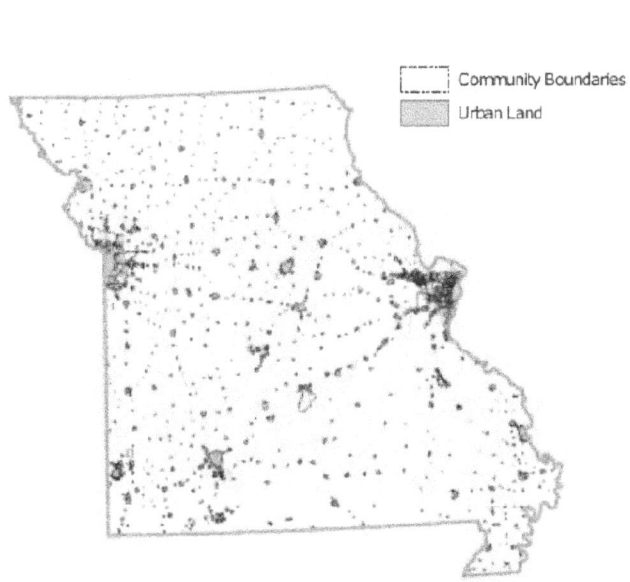

Figure MO-1.—Urban or community land in 2000; urban area relative to community boundaries.

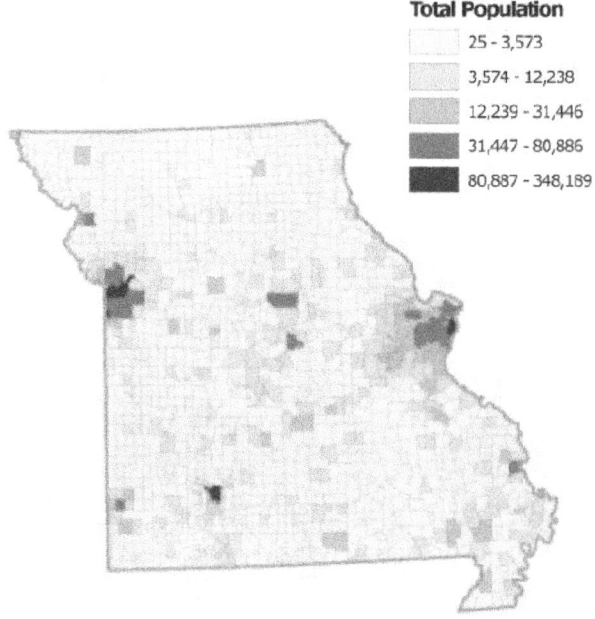

Figure MO-2.—2000 population within county subdivision boundaries.

## Human Population Characteristics and Trends

The population in Missouri increased 9.3 percent, from 5,117,073 in 1990 to 5,595,211 in 2000 (Table MO-1). In Missouri, 69.4 percent of the State's population is in urban areas (Fig. MO-1), and 69.0 percent of the population is within communities (Fig. MO-2).

## Urban and Community Land

Urban land comprises 2.6 percent of the land area of Missouri, while lands within communities make up 4.2 percent of the State (Fig. MO-1). Between 1990 and 2000, urban area increased 12.8 percent, while community land increased from 3.6 to 4.2 percent (Table MO-1). Urban area in Missouri is projected to increase to 6.9 percent by 2050, based on average urban growth pattern of the 1990s (Nowak and Walton 2005). Both urban land (attaining minimum population density) and community land (political boundaries) increased from 1990 to 2000. The percentages are calculated using the total (water and land) area of the geopolitical units derived from U.S. Census cartographic boundary data. Percent urban land varied across the State (Fig. MO-3; Tables MO-2 through 4).

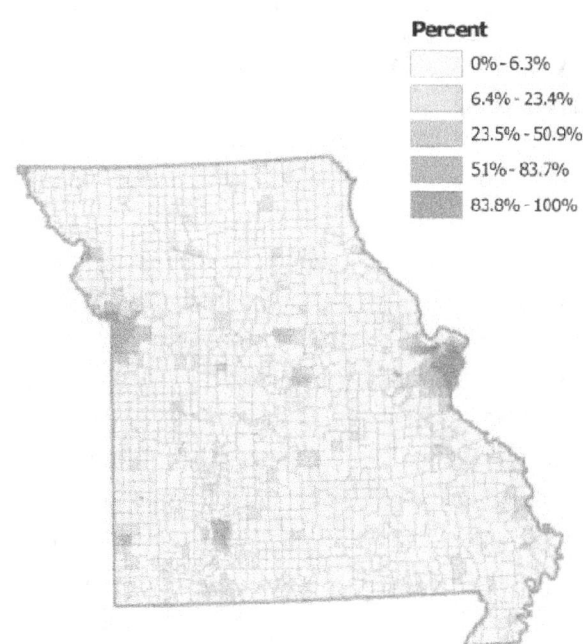

Figure MO-3.—Percent of county subdivision area classified as urban land in 2000.

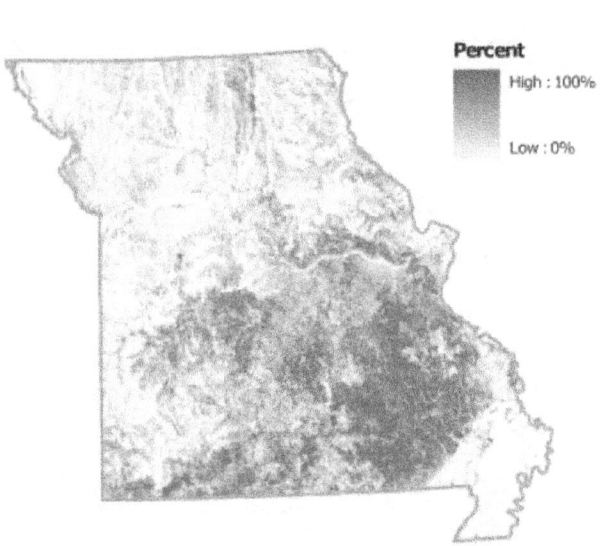

Figure MO-4.—Percentage tree canopy cover.

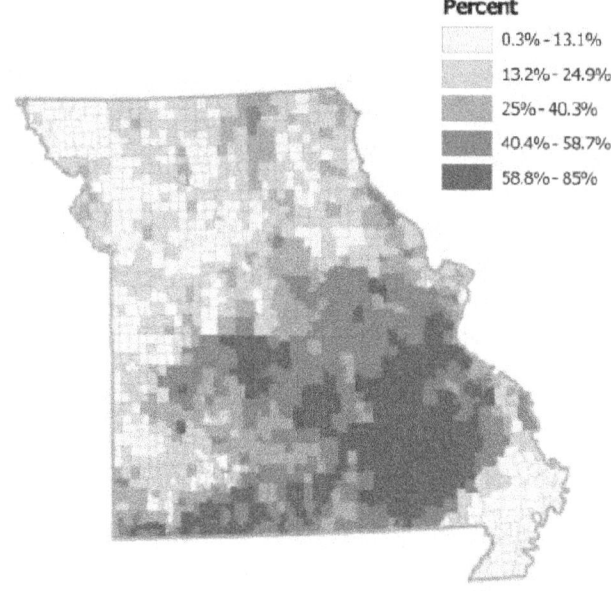

Figure MO-5.—Percentage tree canopy cover within county subdivisions.

## Tree Canopy Cover Characteristics

Tree canopy cover in Missouri averages 32.3 percent (Fig. MO-4), with 98.7 percent total green space, 32.8 percent canopy green space, and 10,285.2 $m^2$ of canopy cover per capita. Average tree cover in urban areas in Missouri was 20.6 percent, with 75.1 percent total green space, 27.4 percent canopy green space, and 248.8 $m^2$ of canopy cover per capita. Within community lands in Missouri, average tree cover was 22.0 percent, with 81.8 percent total green space, 27.0 percent canopy green space, and 424.9 $m^2$ of canopy cover per capita (Table MO-1). Tree canopy cover, canopy green space, and tree cover per capita varied among communities, county subdivisions, and counties (Fig. MO-5 through 6; Tables MO-5 through 7).

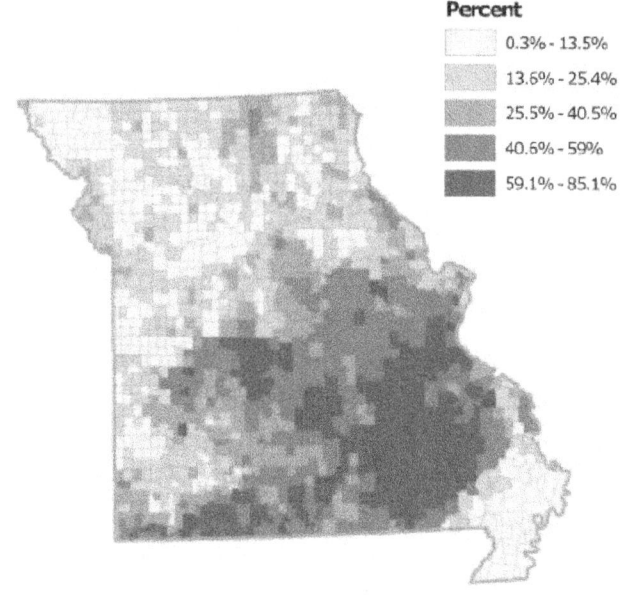

Figure MO-6.—Percentage tree canopy green space in county subdivisions.

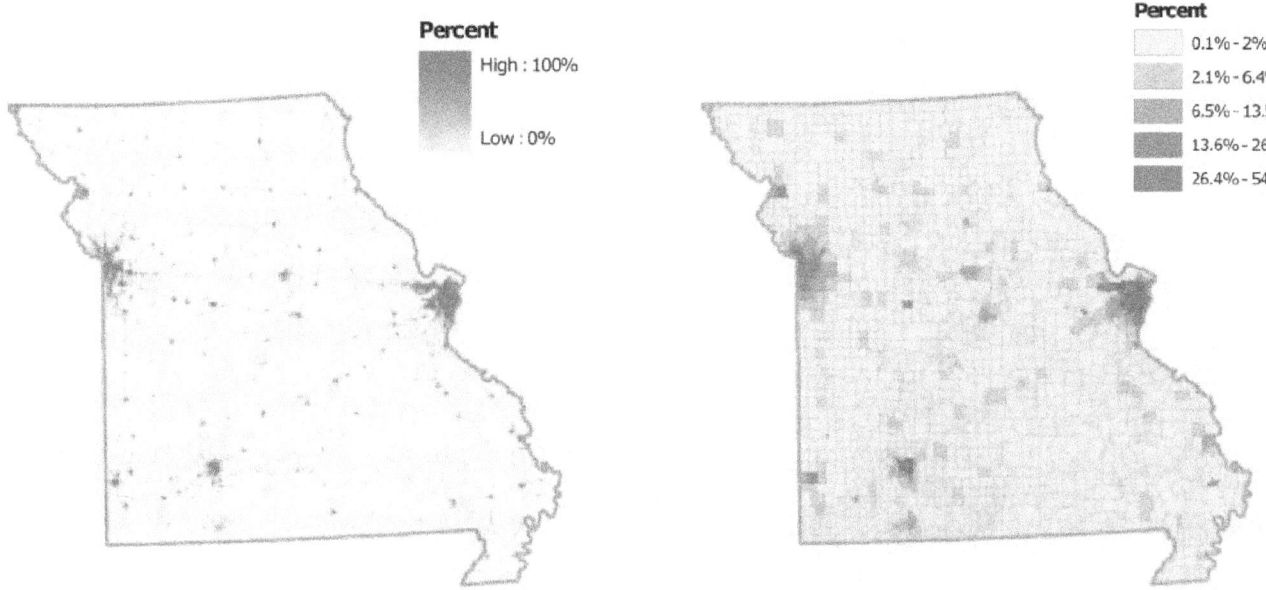

Figure MO-7.—Percentage impervious surface cover.

Figure MO-8.—Percentage impervious surface cover within county subdivisions.

## Impervious Surface Cover Characteristics

Average impervious surface cover in Missouri is 1.3 percent of the land area (Fig. MO-7), with 427.2 $m^2$ of impervious surface cover per capita. Average impervious surface cover in urban areas was 24.9 percent, with 300.6 $m^2$ of impervious surface cover per capita. Within community lands in Missouri, average impervious surface cover was 18.2 percent with 351.4 $m^2$ of impervious surface cover per capita (Table MO-1). Impervious surface cover varied across the State (Fig. MO-8; Tables MO-5 through 7).

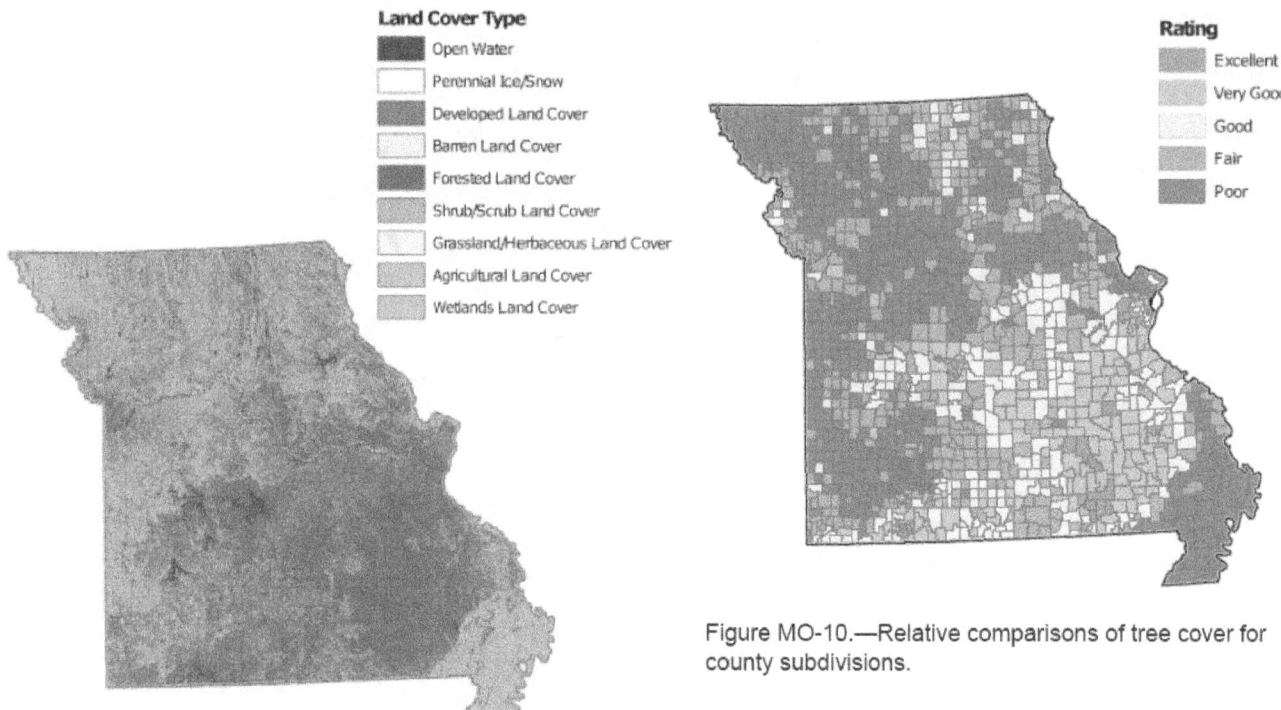

**Land Cover Type**
- Open Water
- Perennial Ice/Snow
- Developed Land Cover
- Barren Land Cover
- Forested Land Cover
- Shrub/Scrub Land Cover
- Grassland/Herbaceous Land Cover
- Agricultural Land Cover
- Wetlands Land Cover

**Rating**
- Excellent
- Very Good
- Good
- Fair
- Poor

Figure MO-10.—Relative comparisons of tree cover for county subdivisions.

Figure MO-9.—Classified land cover.

## Classified Land-cover Characteristics

Missouri's land cover is dominated by agricultural land (Fig. MO-9). The characteristics as a percent of the total land area in Missouri are (Tables MO-8 through 10):

- Agricultural – 53.5 percent
- Forested – 37.4 percent
- Developed – 6.8 percent
- Grassland – 1.5 percent
- Scrub/Shrub – 0.5 percent
- Wetland – 0.2 percent
- Barren – 0.1 percent

## Relative Comparisons of Tree Cover

Out of the 972 Missouri communities, 10 received a rating of excellent and 609 received a rating of poor (Table MO-12). Of the 1,379 county subdivisions, 23 had a rating of excellent and 610 were rated poor (Fig. MO-10, Table MO-13); and out of 115 counties, nine were given a rating of excellent and 29 were given a rating of poor (Table MO-14). Variability of assessment scores is a product of the difference in land cover distributions and the percentage of canopy cover within the population density classes and mapping zones (Fig. MO-10; Tables MO-11 through 14).

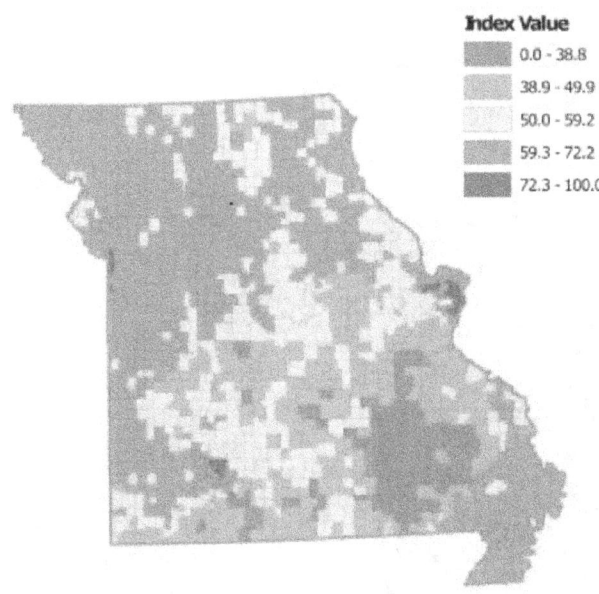

**Index Value**

- 0.0 - 38.8
- 38.9 - 49.9
- 50.0 - 59.2
- 59.3 - 72.2
- 72.3 - 100.0

Figure MO-11.—Planting priority index for county subdivisions. The higher the index value, the greater priority for planting.

## Priority Areas for Tree Planting

Priority areas for planting tend to be highest in more urbanized areas due to higher population density (Fig. MO-11; Tables MO-15 through 17). These index values can also be produced using high resolution cover data to determine local planting priority areas (e.g., neighborhoods).

## Urban Tree Benefits

The following forest attributes are estimated for the urban or community land in Missouri (Table MO-1). These are rough estimates of values. More localized data are needed for more precise estimates, but these values reveal first-order approximations.

- 90.3 million trees
- 17.2 million metric tons of C stored ($392.2 million value)
- 568,000 metric tons/year of C sequestered ($13.0 million value)
- 15,390 metric tons/year total pollution removal ($125.0 million value)
  - 258 metric tons/year of CO removed ($363,500 value)
  - 2,008 metric tons/year $NO_2$ removed ($19.9 million value)
  - 7,022 metric tons/year of $O_3$ removed ($69.6 million value)
  - 1,242 metric tons/year of $SO_2$ removed ($3.0 million value)
  - 4,863 metric tons/year of $PM_{10}$ removed ($32.2 million value)

## Summary

The data presented in this report provide a better understanding of Missouri's urban and community forests. This information can be used to advance urban and community forest policy and management that could improve environmental quality and human health throughout the State.

These data establish a baseline to assess future change and can be used to understand:
- Extent of the urban and community forest resource
- Variations in the resource across the State
- Magnitude and value of the urban and community forest resource
- Urban growth in Missouri
- Implications of policy decisions related to urban sprawl and urban and community forest management

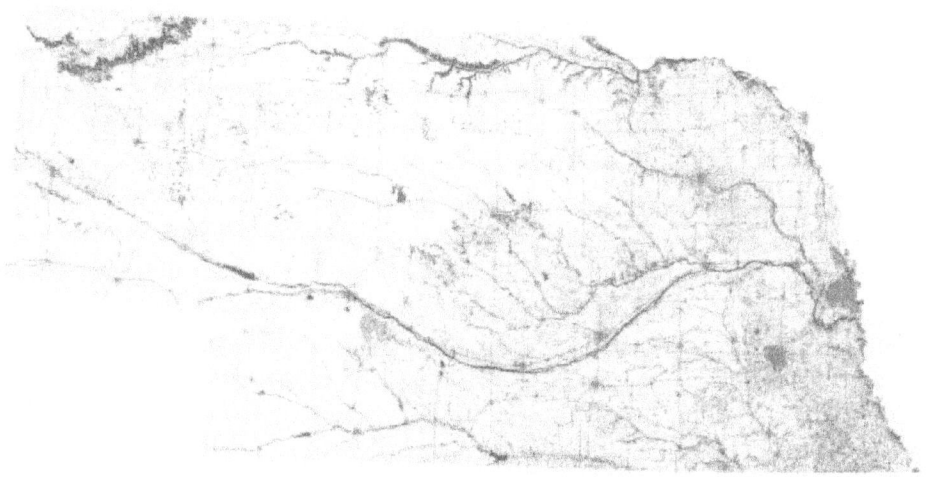

# NEBRASKA'S URBAN
# AND COMMUNITY FORESTS

## Statewide Summary

Urban or community land in Nebraska comprised about 1.0 percent of the
state land area in both 2000 and 1990. Statewide tree canopy cover averages
2.5 percent and tree cover in urban or community areas is about 8.0 percent, with
27.1 percent impervious surface cover and 11.0 percent of the total green space
covered by tree canopy cover. Statewide, urban or community land in Nebraska
has an estimated 7.3 million trees, which store about 1.4 million metric tons of
carbon ($31.9 million), and annually remove about 46,000 metric tons of carbon
($1.0 million) and 1,040 metric tons of air pollution ($8.4 million) (Table NE-1).

Tables NE-2 through NE-17 are not printed in this report but are available on
the CD located on the inside back cover and at http://nrs.fs.fed.us/data/urban.

**Table NE-1.—Statewide summary of population, area, population density, tree canopy and impervious surface land cover, and urban tree benefits in urban, community, and urban or community areas.**

| Nebraska | | Statewide | Urban [a] | Community [b] | Urban or Community [c] |
|---|---|---|---|---|---|
| Population | 2000 | 1,711,263 | 1,193,725 | 1,344,368 | n/a |
| | 1990 | 1,578,385 | 1,043,984 | 1,186,056 | n/a |
| | % Change (1990-2000) | 8.4 | 14.3 | 13.3 | n/a |
| | % Total population (2000) | 100.0 | 69.8 | 78.6 | n/a |
| Total area | km$^2$ (2000) | 200,345.2 | 1,193.6 | 1,662.7 | 1,938.7 |
| | km$^2$ (1990) | 200,345.2 | 1,042.8 | 1,762.8 | 2,011.3 |
| | % Change (1990-2000) | 0.0 | 14.5 | -5.7 | -3.6 |
| Land area | km$^2$ (2000) | 198,379.8 | 1,174.6 | 1,636.0 | 1,906.7 |
| | % Land area (2000) | 100.0 | 0.6 | 0.8 | 1.0 |
| | km$^2$ (1990) | 198,379.8 | 1,028.8 | 1,735.3 | 1,978.7 |
| | % Land area (1990) | 100.0 | 0.5 | 0.9 | 1.0 |
| | % Change (1990-2000) | 0.0 | 14.2 | -5.7 | -3.6 |
| Population density (people/land area km$^2$) | 2000 | 8.6 | 1,016.3 | 821.7 | n/a |
| | 1990 | 8.0 | 1,014.7 | 683.5 | n/a |
| | % Change (1990-2000) | 8.4 | 0.2 | 20.2 | n/a |
| Tree canopy cover (2000) | km$^2$ | 4,919.8 | 100.7 | 131.9 | 152.9 |
| | % Land area | 2.5 | 8.6 | 8.1 | 8.0 |
| | Per capita (m$^2$/person) | 2,875.0 | 84.4 | 98.1 | n/a |
| | % Canopy green space [d] | 2.5 | 12.6 | 11.4 | 11.0 |
| Total green space (2000) [e] | km$^2$ | 197,192.0 | 799.3 | 1,155.8 | 1,390.3 |
| | % Land area | 99.4 | 68.0 | 70.6 | 72.9 |
| Available green space (2000) [f] | km$^2$ | 192,272.0 | 698.7 | 1,024.0 | 1,237.6 |
| | % Land area | 96.9 | 59.5 | 62.6 | 64.9 |
| Impervious surface cover (2000) | km$^2$ | 1,188.2 | 375.3 | 480.2 | 516.4 |
| | % Land area | 0.6 | 32.0 | 29.4 | 27.1 |
| | Per capita (m$^2$/person) | 694.3 | 314.4 | 357.2 | n/a |
| Urban tree benefits (2000) | Estimated number of trees | n/a | 4,800,000 | 6,300,000 | 7,300,000 |
| | **Carbon** | | | | |
| | Carbon stored (metric tons) | n/a | 900,000 | 1,200,000 | 1,400,000 |
| | Carbon stored ($) | n/a | $20,500,000 | $27,400,000 | $31,900,000 |
| | Carbon sequestered (metric tons/year) | n/a | 30,000 | 40,000 | 46,000 |
| | Carbon sequestered ($/year) | n/a | $684,000 | $912,000 | $1,049,000 |
| | **Pollution** | | | | |
| | CO removed (metric tons/year) | n/a | 12 | 15 | 18 |
| | CO removed ($/year) | n/a | $16,200 | $21,200 | $24,600 |
| | NO$_2$ removed (metric tons/year) | n/a | 122 | 160 | 186 |
| | NO$_2$ removed ($/year) | n/a | $1,212,400 | $1,588,200 | $1,841,300 |
| | O$_3$ removed (metric tons/year) | n/a | 263 | 345 | 400 |
| | O$_3$ removed ($/year) | n/a | $2,606,000 | $3,415,000 | $3,959,000 |
| | SO$_2$ removed (metric tons/year) | n/a | 41 | 53 | 62 |
| | SO$_2$ removed ($/year) | n/a | $98,900 | $129,600 | $150,200 |
| | PM$_{10}$ removed (metric tons/year) | n/a | 245 | 321 | 372 |
| | PM$_{10}$ removed ($/year) | n/a | $1,620,000 | $2,122,300 | $2,460,400 |
| | Total pollution removal (metric tons/year) | n/a | 680 | 890 | 1,040 |
| | Total pollution removal ($/year) | n/a | $5,600,000 | $7,300,000 | $8,400,000 |

[a] Urban land is based on population density and was delimited using the United States Census definitions of urbanized areas and urban clusters. [b] Community land is based on jurisdictional or political boundaries of communities based on United States Census definitions of incorporated or census designated places. [c] Urban or communities is land that is urban, community, or both. Communities may include all, some, or no urban land within their boundaries. [d] Canopy green space is the tree canopy cover divided by total green space. [e] Total green space (TGS) is total area – impervious surface cover – water. [f] Available green space (AGS) is total green space – tree canopy cover (if the calculated value is less than 0, then value set at 0).

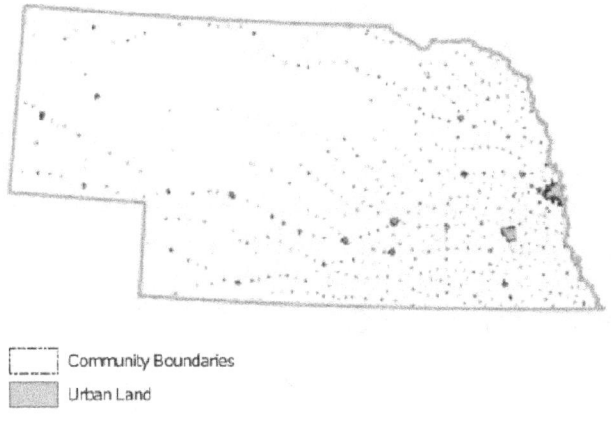

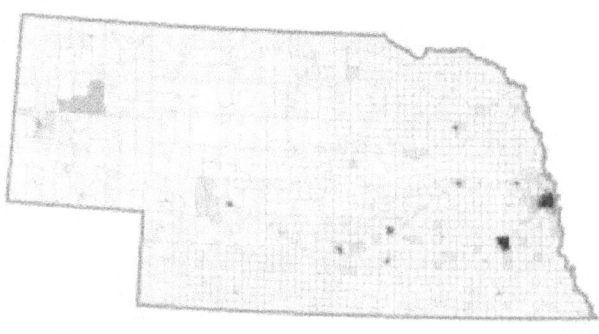

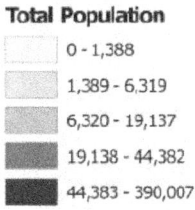

Community Boundaries

Urban Land

Figure NE-1.—Urban or community land in 2000;
urban area relative to community boundaries.

**Total Population**

0 - 1,388

1,389 - 6,319

6,320 - 19,137

19,138 - 44,382

44,383 - 390,007

Figure NE-2.—2000 population within county
subdivision boundaries.

## Human Population Characteristics and Trends

The population in Nebraska increased 8.4 percent, from
1,578,385 in 1990 to 1,711,263 in 2000 (Table NE-1).
In Nebraska, 69.8 percent of the State's population
is in urban areas (Fig. NE-1), and 78.6 percent of the
population is within communities (Fig. NE-2).

## Urban and Community Land

Urban land comprises 0.6 percent of the land area of
Nebraska, while lands within communities make up
0.8 percent of the State (Fig. NE-1). Between 1990
and 2000, urban area increased 14.2 percent, while
community land decreased from 0.9 to 0.8 percent
(Table NE-1). Urban area in Nebraska is projected to
increase to 1.8 percent by 2050, based on average urban
growth pattern of the 1990s (Nowak and Walton 2005).
Urban land (attaining minimum population density)
increased and community land (political boundaries)
decreased from 1990 to 2000. The percentages are
calculated using the total (water and land) area of the
geopolitical units derived from U.S. Census cartographic
boundary data. Percent urban land varied across the State
(Fig. NE-3; Tables NE-2 through 4).

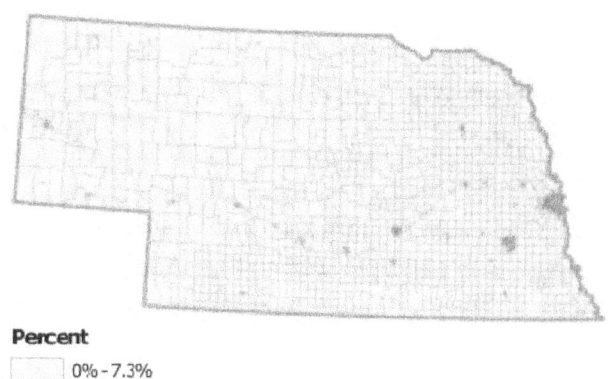

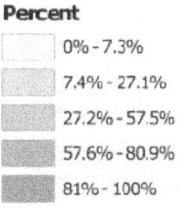

**Percent**

0% - 7.3%

7.4% - 27.1%

27.2% - 57.5%

57.6% - 80.9%

81% - 100%

Figure NE-3.—Percent of county subdivision area
classified as urban land in 2000.

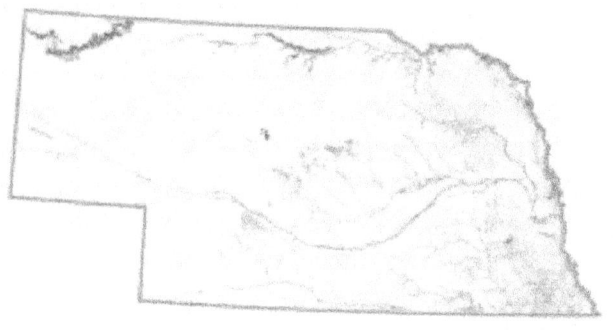

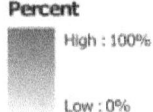

Figure NE-4.—Percentage tree canopy cover.

**Percent**

| | |
|---|---|
| | 0% - 2.7% |
| | 2.8% - 6.9% |
| | 7% - 14.1% |
| | 14.2% - 28.8% |
| | 28.9% - 59.1% |

Figure NE-5.—Percentage tree canopy cover within county subdivisions.

## Tree Canopy Cover Characteristics

Tree canopy cover in Nebraska averages 2.5 percent (Fig. NE-4), with 99.4 percent total green space, 2.5 percent canopy green space, and 2,875.0 m² of canopy cover per capita. Average tree cover in urban areas in Nebraska was 8.6 percent, with 68.0 percent total green space, 12.6 percent canopy green space, and 84.4 m² of canopy cover per capita. Within community lands in Nebraska, average tree cover was 8.1 percent, with 70.6 percent total green space, 11.4 percent canopy green space, and 98.1 m² of canopy cover per capita (Table NE-1). Tree canopy cover, canopy green space, and tree cover per capita varied among communities, county subdivisions, and counties (Fig. NE-5 through 6; Tables NE-5 through 7).

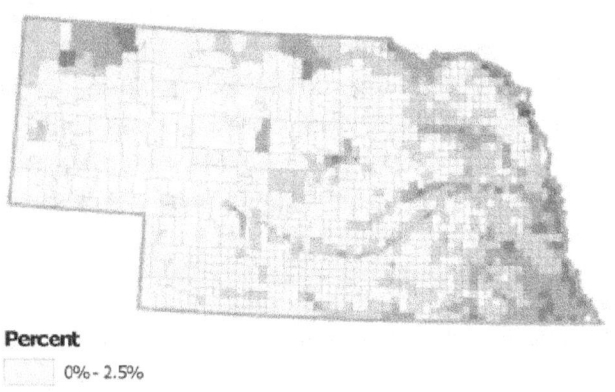

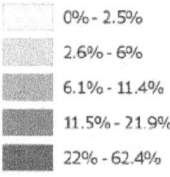

**Percent**

| | |
|---|---|
| | 0% - 2.5% |
| | 2.6% - 6% |
| | 6.1% - 11.4% |
| | 11.5% - 21.9% |
| | 22% - 62.4% |

Figure NE-6.—Percentage tree canopy green space in county subdivisions.

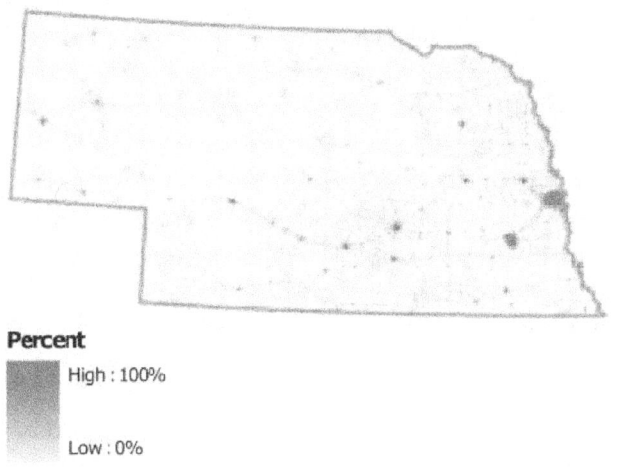

**Percent**

High : 100%

Low : 0%

Figure NE-7.—Percentage impervious surface cover.

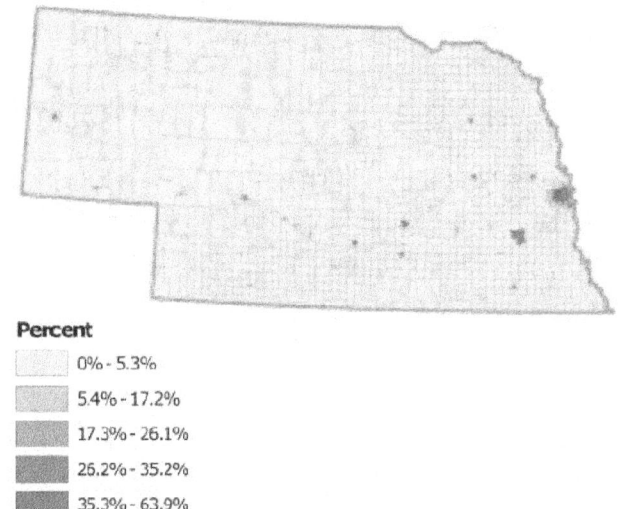

**Percent**

0% - 5.3%

5.4% - 17.2%

17.3% - 26.1%

26.2% - 35.2%

35.3% - 63.9%

Figure NE-8.—Percentage impervious surface cover within county subdivisions.

## Impervious Surface Cover Characteristics

Average impervious surface cover in Nebraska is 0.6 percent of the land area (Fig. NE-7), with 694.3 $m^2$ of impervious surface cover per capita. Average impervious surface cover in urban areas was 32.0 percent, with 314.4 $m^2$ of impervious surface cover per capita. Within community lands in Nebraska, average impervious surface cover was 29.4 percent with 357.2 $m^2$ of impervious surface cover per capita (Table NE-1). Impervious surface cover varied across the State (Fig. NE-8; Tables NE-5 through 7).

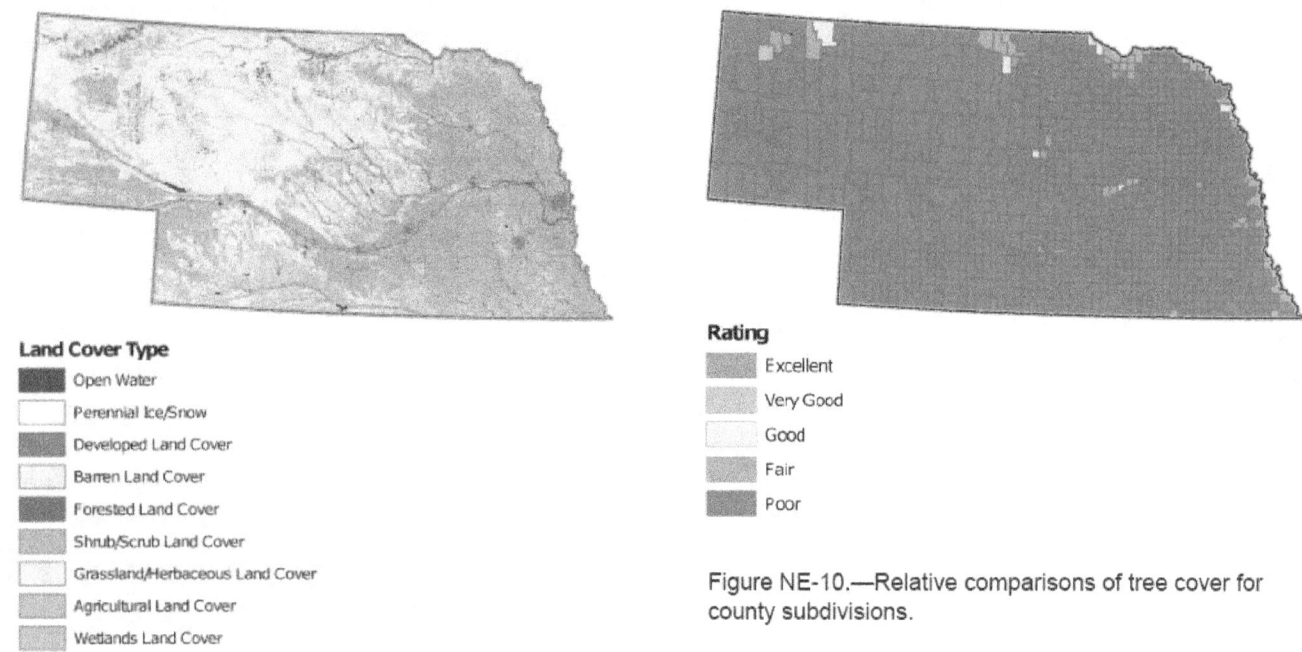

**Land Cover Type**
- Open Water
- Perennial Ice/Snow
- Developed Land Cover
- Barren Land Cover
- Forested Land Cover
- Shrub/Scrub Land Cover
- Grassland/Herbaceous Land Cover
- Agricultural Land Cover
- Wetlands Land Cover

Figure NE-9.—Classified land cover.

**Rating**
- Excellent
- Very Good
- Good
- Fair
- Poor

Figure NE-10.—Relative comparisons of tree cover for county subdivisions.

## Classified Land-cover Characteristics

Nebraska's land cover is dominated by grassland (Fig. NE-9). The characteristics as a percent of the total land area in Nebraska are (Tables NE-8 through 10):
- Grassland – 54.7 percent
- Agricultural – 38.2 percent
- Developed – 3.6 percent
- Forested – 2.0 percent
- Wetland – 1.4 percent
- Scrub/Shrub – 0.1 percent
- Barren – 0.1 percent

## Relative Comparisons of Tree Cover

Out of the 537 Nebraska communities, nine received a rating of excellent and 362 received a rating of poor (Table NE-12). Of the 1,234 county subdivisions, 15 had a rating of excellent and 1,118 were rated poor (Fig. NE-10, Table NE-13); and out of 93 counties, one was given a rating of excellent and 60 were given a rating of poor (Table NE-14). Variability of assessment scores is a product of the difference in land cover distributions and the percentage of canopy cover within the population density classes and mapping zones (Fig. NE-10; Tables NE-11 through 14).

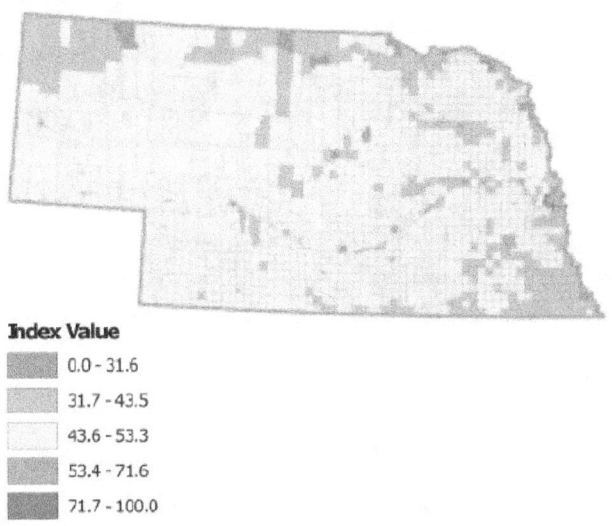

**Index Value**

- 0.0 - 31.6
- 31.7 - 43.5
- 43.6 - 53.3
- 53.4 - 71.6
- 71.7 - 100.0

Figure NE-11.—Planting priority index for county subdivisions. The higher the index value, the greater priority for planting.

## Priority Areas for Tree Planting

Priority areas for planting tend to be highest in more urbanized areas due to higher population density (Fig. NE-11; Tables NE-15 through 17). These index values can also be produced using high resolution cover data to determine local planting priority areas (e.g., neighborhoods).

## Urban Tree Benefits

The following forest attributes are estimated for the urban or community land in Nebraska (Table NE-1). These are rough estimates of values. More localized data are needed for more precise estimates, but these values reveal first-order approximations.

- 7.3 million trees
- 1.4 million metric tons of C stored ($31.9 million value)
- 46,000 metric tons/year of C sequestered ($1.0 million value)
- 1,040 metric tons/year total pollution removal ($8.4 million value)
  - 18 metric tons/year of CO removed ($24,600 value)
  - 186 metric tons/year $NO_2$ removed ($1.8 million value)
  - 400 metric tons/year of $O_3$ removed ($4.0 million value)
  - 62 metric tons/year of $SO_2$ removed ($150,200 value)
  - 372 metric tons/year of $PM_{10}$ removed ($2.5 million value)

## Summary

The data presented in this report provide a better understanding of Nebraska's urban and community forests. This information can be used to advance urban and community forest policy and management that could improve environmental quality and human health throughout the State.

These data establish a baseline to assess future change and can be used to understand:
- Extent of the urban and community forest resource
- Variations in the resource across the State
- Magnitude and value of the urban and community forest resource
- Urban growth in Nebraska
- Implications of policy decisions related to urban sprawl and urban and community forest management

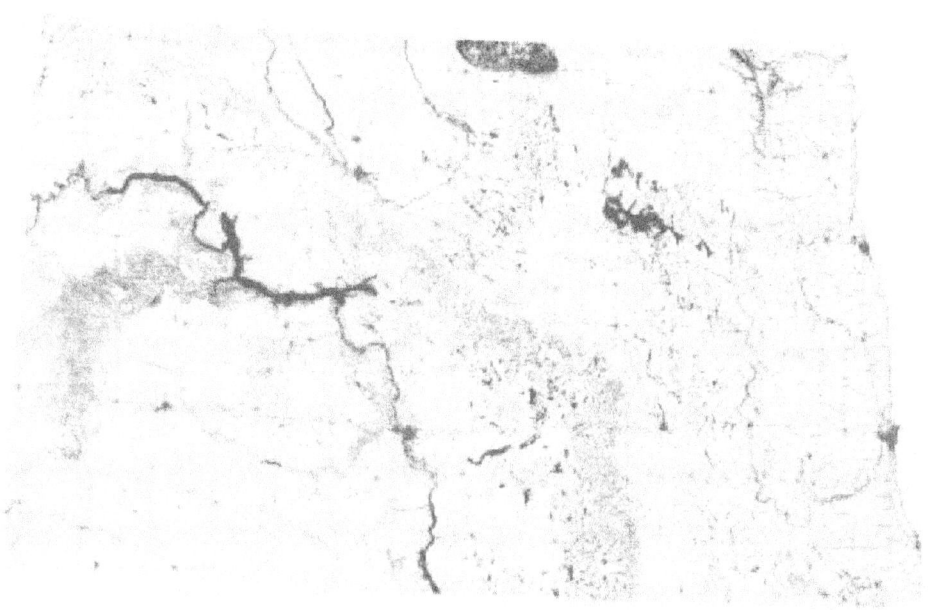

# NORTH DAKOTA'S URBAN AND COMMUNITY FORESTS

## Statewide Summary

Urban or community land in North Dakota comprised about 0.9 percent of the state land area in both 2000 and 1990. Statewide tree canopy cover averages 1.6 percent and tree cover in urban or community areas is about 2.5 percent, with 12.2 percent impervious surface cover and 2.9 percent of the total green space covered by tree canopy cover. Statewide, urban or community land in North Dakota has an estimated 1.9 million trees, which store about 400,000 metric tons of carbon ($9.1 million), and annually remove about 12,000 metric tons of carbon ($274,000) and 210 metric tons of air pollution ($1.9 million) (Table ND-1).

Tables ND-2 through ND-17 are not printed in this report but are available on the CD located on the inside back cover and at http://nrs.fs.fed.us/data/urban.

**Table ND-1.—Statewide summary of population, area, population density, tree canopy and impervious surface land cover, and urban tree benefits in urban, community, and urban or community areas.**

| North Dakota | | Statewide | Urban [a] | Community [b] | Urban or Community [c] |
|---|---|---|---|---|---|
| Population | 2000 | 642,200 | 358,958 | 486,511 | n/a |
| | 1990 | 638,800 | 340,339 | 473,323 | n/a |
| | % Change (1990-2000) | 0.5 | 5.5 | 2.8 | n/a |
| | % Total population (2000) | 100.0 | 55.9 | 75.8 | n/a |
| Total area | km$^2$ (2000) | 183,111.6 | 378.4 | 1,617.8 | 1,664.5 |
| | km$^2$ (1990) | 183,111.6 | 345.6 | 1,531.2 | 1,586.9 |
| | % Change (1990-2000) | 0.0 | 9.5 | 5.7 | 4.9 |
| Land area | km$^2$ (2000) | 176,157.8 | 373.0 | 1,555.6 | 1,601.3 |
| | % Land area (2000) | 100.0 | 0.2 | 0.9 | 0.9 |
| | km$^2$ (1990) | 176,157.8 | 341.0 | 1,472.4 | 1,526.9 |
| | % Land area (1990) | 100.0 | 0.2 | 0.8 | 0.9 |
| | % Change (1990-2000) | 0.0 | 9.4 | 5.7 | 4.9 |
| Population density (people/land area km$^2$) | 2000 | 3.6 | 962.2 | 312.7 | n/a |
| | 1990 | 3.6 | 998.2 | 321.5 | n/a |
| | % Change (1990-2000) | 0.5 | -3.6 | -2.7 | n/a |
| Tree canopy cover (2000) | km$^2$ | 2,759.7 | 16.6 | 38.8 | 40.8 |
| | % Land area | 1.6 | 4.5 | 2.5 | 2.5 |
| | Per capita (m$^2$/person) | 4,297.2 | 46.3 | 79.8 | n/a |
| | % Canopy green space [d] | 1.6 | 6.3 | 2.8 | 2.9 |
| Total green space (2000) [e] | km$^2$ | 175,400.0 | 265.6 | 1,362.9 | 1,405.2 |
| | % Land area | 99.6 | 71.2 | 87.6 | 87.8 |
| Available green space (2000) [f] | km$^2$ | 172,641.0 | 249.0 | 1,324.1 | 1,364.4 |
| | % Land area | 98.0 | 66.8 | 85.1 | 85.2 |
| Impervious surface cover (2000) | km$^2$ | 757.5 | 107.4 | 192.7 | 196.1 |
| | % Land area | 0.4 | 28.8 | 12.4 | 12.2 |
| | Per capita (m$^2$/person) | 1,179.5 | 299.2 | 396.1 | n/a |
| Urban tree benefits (2000) | Estimated number of trees | n/a | 800,000 | 1,900,000 | 1,900,000 |
| | **Carbon** | | | | |
| | Carbon stored (metric tons) | n/a | 200,000 | 400,000 | 400,000 |
| | Carbon stored ($) | n/a | $4,600,000 | $9,100,000 | $9,100,000 |
| | Carbon sequestered (metric tons/year) | n/a | 5,000 | 12,000 | 12,000 |
| | Carbon sequestered ($/year) | n/a | $114,000 | $274,000 | $274,000 |
| | **Pollution** | | | | |
| | CO removed (metric tons/year) | n/a | 3 | 6 | 7 |
| | CO removed ($/year) | n/a | $3,900 | $9,100 | $9,500 |
| | NO$_2$ removed (metric tons/year) | n/a | 4 | 10 | 11 |
| | NO$_2$ removed ($/year) | n/a | $44,000 | $102,900 | $108,100 |
| | O$_3$ removed (metric tons/year) | n/a | 65 | 153 | 161 |
| | O$_3$ removed ($/year) | n/a | $648,000 | $1,515,000 | $1,592,000 |
| | SO$_2$ removed (metric tons/year) | n/a | 3 | 6 | 6 |
| | SO$_2$ removed ($/year) | n/a | $6,300 | $14,800 | $15,600 |
| | PM$_{10}$ removed (metric tons/year) | n/a | 12 | 28 | 30 |
| | PM$_{10}$ removed ($/year) | n/a | $80,600 | $188,500 | $198,000 |
| | Total pollution removal (metric tons/year) | n/a | 90 | 200 | 210 |
| | Total pollution removal ($/year) | n/a | $800,000 | $1,800,000 | $1,900,000 |

[a] Urban land is based on population density and was delimited using the United States Census definitions of urbanized areas and urban clusters. [b] Community land is based on jurisdictional or political boundaries of communities based on United States Census definitions of incorporated or census designated places. [c] Urban or communities is land that is urban, community, or both. Communities may include all, some, or no urban land within their boundaries. [d] Canopy green space is the tree canopy cover divided by total green space. [e] Total green space (TGS) is total area – impervious surface cover – water. [f] Available green space (AGS) is total green space – tree canopy cover (if the calculated value is less than 0, then value set at 0).

Community Boundaries

Urban Land

Figure ND-1.—Urban or community land in 2000; urban area relative to community boundaries.

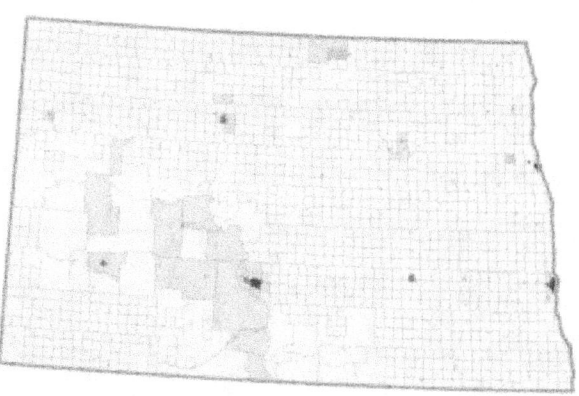

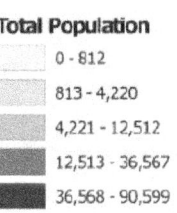

**Total Population**

0 - 812

813 - 4,220

4,221 - 12,512

12,513 - 36,567

36,568 - 90,599

Figure ND-2.—2000 population within county subdivision boundaries.

## Human Population Characteristics and Trends

The population in North Dakota increased 0.5 percent, from 638,800 in 1990 to 642,200 in 2000 (Table ND-1). In North Dakota, 55.9 percent of the State's population is in urban areas (Fig. ND-1), and 75.8 percent of the population is within communities (Fig. ND-2).

## Urban and Community Land

Urban land comprises 0.2 percent of the land area of North Dakota, while lands within communities make up 0.9 percent of the State (Fig. ND-1). Between 1990 and 2000, urban area increased 9.4 percent, while community land increased from 0.8 to 0.9 percent (Table ND-1). Urban area in North Dakota is projected to increase to 1.0 percent by 2050, based on average urban growth pattern of the 1990s (Nowak and Walton 2005). Both urban land (attaining minimum population density) and community land (political boundaries) increased from 1990 to 2000. The percentages are calculated using the total (water and land) area of the geopolitical units derived from U.S. Census cartographic boundary data. Percent urban land varied across the State (Fig. ND-3; Tables ND-2 through 4).

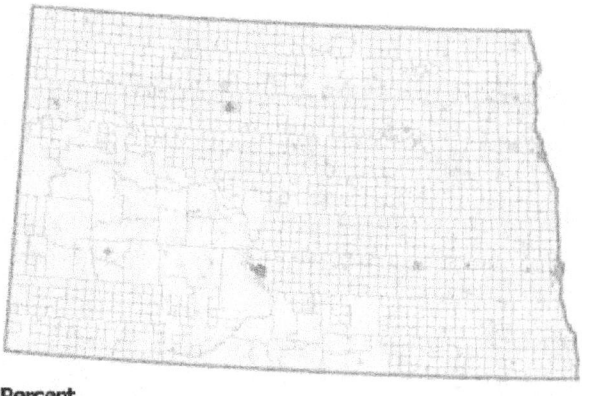

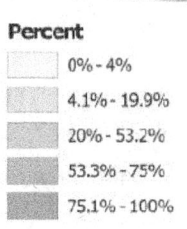

**Percent**

0% - 4%

4.1% - 19.9%

20% - 53.2%

53.3% - 75%

75.1% - 100%

Figure ND-3.—Percent of county subdivision area classified as urban land in 2000.

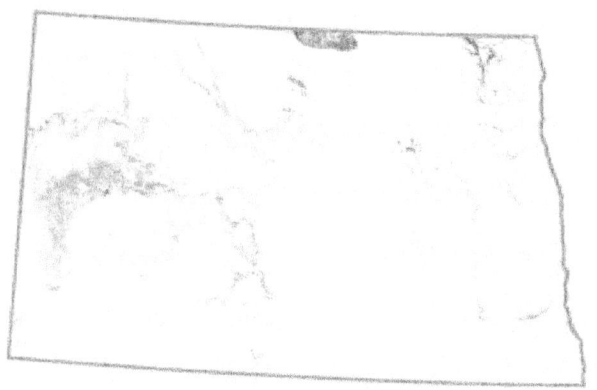

Figure ND-4.—Percentage tree canopy cover.

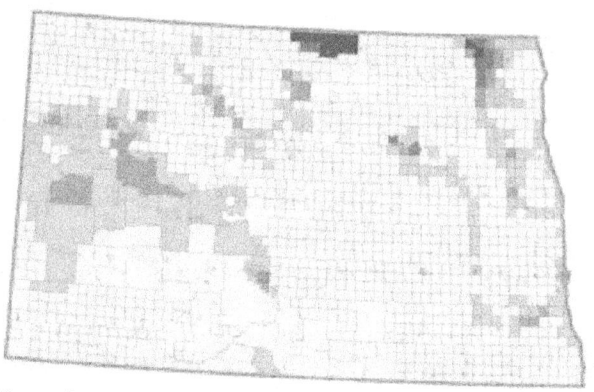

**Percent**

0% - 1.7%

1.8% - 5.1%

5.2% - 11.2%

11.3% - 26.5%

26.6% - 48.2%

Figure ND-5.—Percentage tree canopy cover within county subdivisions.

## Tree Canopy Cover Characteristics

Tree canopy cover in North Dakota averages 1.6 percent (Fig. ND-4), with 99.6 percent total green space, 1.6 percent canopy green space, and 4,297.2 m² of canopy cover per capita. Average tree cover in urban areas in North Dakota was 4.5 percent, with 71.2 percent total green space, 6.3 percent canopy green space, and 46.3 m² of canopy cover per capita. Within community lands in North Dakota, average tree cover was 2.5 percent, with 87.6 percent total green space, 2.8 percent canopy green space, and 79.8 m² of canopy cover per capita (Table ND-1). Tree canopy cover, canopy green space, and tree cover per capita varied among communities, county subdivisions, and counties (Fig. ND-5 through 6; Tables ND-5 through 7).

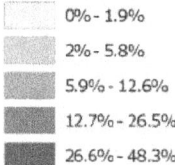

**Percent**

0% - 1.9%

2% - 5.8%

5.9% - 12.6%

12.7% - 26.5%

26.6% - 48.3%

Figure ND-6.—Percentage tree canopy green space in county subdivisions.

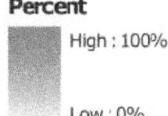
Figure ND-7.—Percentage impervious surface cover.

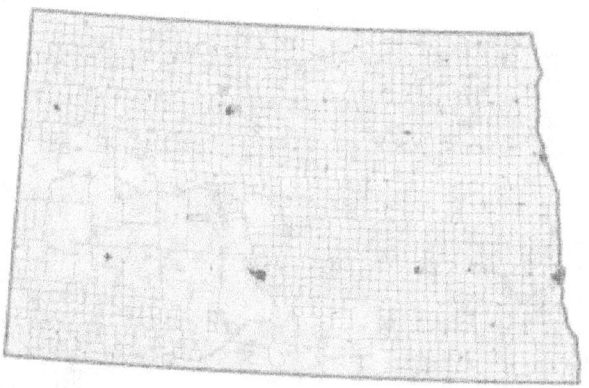

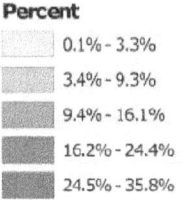
Figure ND-8.—Percentage impervious surface cover within county subdivisions.

## Impervious Surface Cover Characteristics

Average impervious surface cover in North Dakota is 0.4 percent of the land area (Fig. ND-7), with 1,179.5 $m^2$ of impervious surface cover per capita. Average impervious surface cover in urban areas was 28.8 percent, with 299.2 $m^2$ of impervious surface cover per capita. Within community lands in North Dakota, average impervious surface cover was 12.4 percent with 396.1 $m^2$ of impervious surface cover per capita (Table ND-1). Impervious surface cover varied across the State (Fig. ND-8; Tables ND-5 through 7).

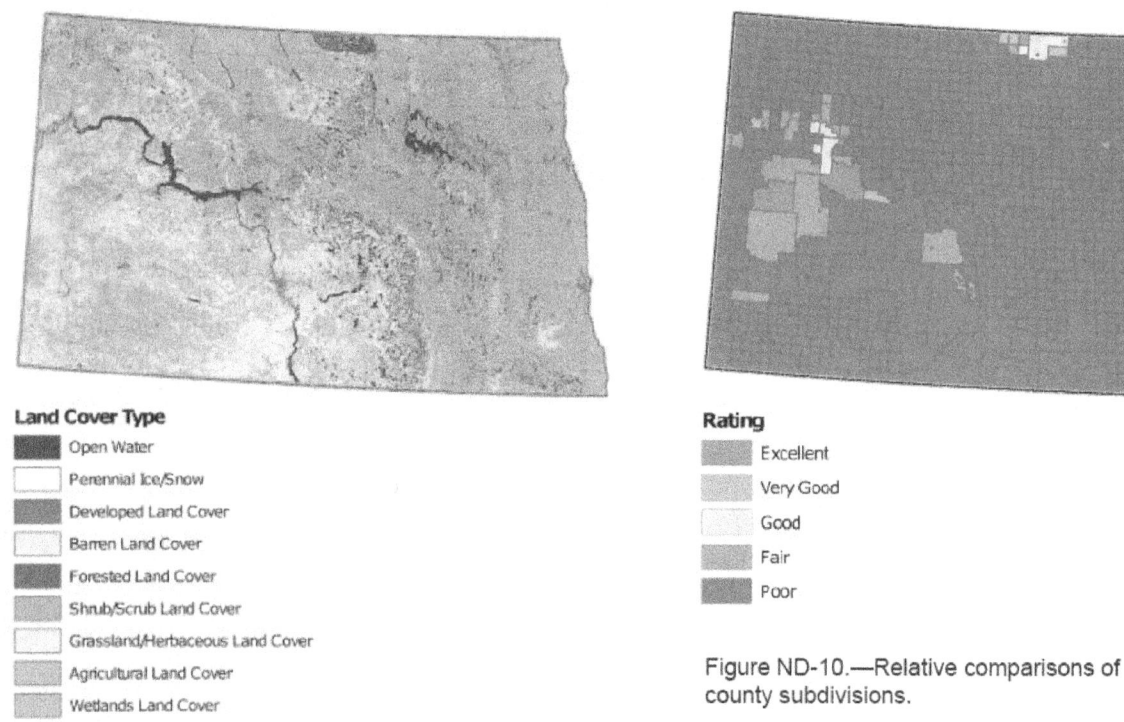

**Land Cover Type**
- Open Water
- Perennial Ice/Snow
- Developed Land Cover
- Barren Land Cover
- Forested Land Cover
- Shrub/Scrub Land Cover
- Grassland/Herbaceous Land Cover
- Agricultural Land Cover
- Wetlands Land Cover

**Rating**
- Excellent
- Very Good
- Good
- Fair
- Poor

Figure ND-10.—Relative comparisons of tree cover for county subdivisions.

Figure ND-9.—Classified land cover.

## Classified Land-cover Characteristics

North Dakota's land cover is dominated by agricultural land (Fig. ND-9). The characteristics as a percent of the total land area in North Dakota are (Tables ND-8 through 10):

- Agricultural – 57.9 percent
- Grassland – 30.9 percent
- Developed – 4.1 percent
- Wetland – 3.9 percent
- Forested – 1.8 percent
- Scrub/Shrub – 1.1 percent
- Barren – 0.2 percent

## Relative Comparisons of Tree Cover

Out of the 373 North Dakota communities, nine received a rating of excellent and 325 received a rating of poor (Table ND-12). Of the 1,790 county subdivisions, 11 had a rating of excellent and 1,706 were rated poor (Fig. ND-10, Table ND-13); and out of 53 counties, two were given a rating of excellent and 45 were given a rating of poor (Table ND-14). Variability of assessment scores is a product of the difference in land cover distributions and the percentage of canopy cover within the population density classes and mapping zones (Fig. ND-10; Tables ND-11 through 14).

Index Value

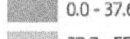

- 0.0 - 37.6
- 37.7 - 55.5
- 55.6 - 63.5
- 63.6 - 73.1
- 73.2 - 100.0

Figure ND-11.—Planting priority index for county subdivisions. The higher the index value, the greater priority for planting.

## Priority Areas for Tree Planting

Priority areas for planting tend to be highest in more urbanized areas due to higher population density (Fig. ND-11; Tables ND-15 through 17). These index values can also be produced using high resolution cover data to determine local planting priority areas (e.g., neighborhoods).

## Urban Tree Benefits

The following forest attributes are estimated for the urban or community land in North Dakota (Table ND-1). These are rough estimates of values. More localized data are needed for more precise estimates, but these values reveal first-order approximations.

- 1.9 million trees
- 400,000 metric tons of C stored ($9.1 million value)
- 12,000 metric tons/year of C sequestered ($274,000 value)
- 210 metric tons/year total pollution removal ($1.9 million value)
  - 7 metric tons/year of CO removed ($9,500 value)
  - 11 metric tons/year $NO_2$ removed ($108,100 million value)
  - 161 metric tons/year of $O_3$ removed ($1.6 million value)
  - 6 metric tons/year of $SO_2$ removed ($15,600 value)
  - 30 metric tons/year of $PM_{10}$ removed ($198,000 value)

## Summary

The data presented in this report provide a better understanding of North Dakota's urban and community forests. This information can be used to advance urban and community forest policy and management that could improve environmental quality and human health throughout the State.

These data establish a baseline to assess future change and can be used to understand:
- Extent of the urban and community forest resource
- Variations in the resource across the State
- Magnitude and value of the urban and community forest resource
- Urban growth in North Dakota
- Implications of policy decisions related to urban sprawl and urban and community forest management

# SOUTH DAKOTA'S URBAN AND COMMUNITY FORESTS

## Statewide Summary

Urban or community land in South Dakota comprises about 0.9 percent of the state land area in 2000, an increase from 0.7 percent in 1990. Statewide tree canopy cover averages 2.3 percent and tree cover in urban or community areas is about 4.6 percent, with 12.7 percent impervious surface cover and 5.3 percent of the total green space covered by tree canopy cover. Statewide, urban or community land in South Dakota has an estimated 3.8 million trees, which store about 700,000 metric tons of carbon ($16.0 million), and annually remove about 24,000 metric tons of carbon ($547,000 million) and 450 metric tons of air pollution ($4.0 million) (Table SD-1).

Tables SD-2 through SD-17 are not printed in this report but are available on the CD located on the inside back cover and at http://nrs.fs.fed.us/data/urban.

**Table SD-1.—Statewide summary of population, area, population density, tree canopy and impervious surface land cover, and urban tree benefits in urban, community, and urban or community areas.**

| South Dakota | | Statewide | Urban [a] | Community [b] | Urban or Community [c] |
|---|---|---|---|---|---|
| Population | 2000 | 754,844 | 391,427 | 540,667 | n/a |
| | 1990 | 696,004 | 347,903 | 488,304 | n/a |
| | % Change (1990-2000) | 8.5 | 12.5 | 10.7 | n/a |
| | % Total population (2000) | 100.0 | 51.9 | 71.6 | n/a |
| Total area | km$^2$ (2000) | 199,730.8 | 436.2 | 1,701.2 | 1,749.2 |
| | km$^2$ (1990) | 199,730.8 | 396.5 | 1,347.7 | 1,400.6 |
| | % Change (1990-2000) | 0.0 | 10.0 | 26.2 | 24.9 |
| Land area | km$^2$ (2000) | 194,872.1 | 432.7 | 1,645.8 | 1,693.1 |
| | % Land area (2000) | 100.0 | 0.2 | 0.8 | 0.9 |
| | km$^2$ (1990) | 194,872.1 | 394.1 | 1,298.4 | 1,350.7 |
| | % Land area (1990) | 100.0 | 0.2 | 0.7 | 0.7 |
| | % Change (1990-2000) | 0.0 | 9.8 | 26.8 | 25.4 |
| Population density (people/land area km$^2$) | 2000 | 3.9 | 904.7 | 328.5 | n/a |
| | 1990 | 3.6 | 882.8 | 376.1 | n/a |
| | % Change (1990-2000) | 8.5 | 2.5 | -12.6 | n/a |
| Tree canopy cover (2000) | km$^2$ | 4,434.9 | 30.0 | 75.6 | 78.7 |
| | % Land area | 2.3 | 6.9 | 4.6 | 4.6 |
| | Per capita (m$^2$/person) | 5,875.3 | 76.6 | 139.8 | n/a |
| | % Canopy green space [d] | 2.3 | 9.5 | 5.3 | 5.3 |
| Total green space (2000) [e] | km$^2$ | 194,156.0 | 315.0 | 1,433.5 | 1,477.7 |
| | % Land area | 99.6 | 72.8 | 87.1 | 87.3 |
| Available green space (2000) [f] | km$^2$ | 189,721.0 | 285.0 | 1,357.9 | 1,399.0 |
| | % Land area | 97.4 | 65.9 | 82.5 | 82.6 |
| Impervious surface cover (2000) | km$^2$ | 716.5 | 117.7 | 212.2 | 215.4 |
| | % Land area | 0.4 | 27.2 | 12.9 | 12.7 |
| | Per capita (m$^2$/person) | 949.2 | 300.6 | 392.6 | n/a |
| Urban tree benefits (2000) | Estimated number of trees | n/a | 1,400,000 | 3,600,000 | 3,800,000 |
| | **Carbon** | | | | |
| | Carbon stored (metric tons) | n/a | 300,000 | 700,000 | 700,000 |
| | Carbon stored ($) | n/a | $6,800,000 | $16,000,000 | $16,000,000 |
| | Carbon sequestered (metric tons/year) | n/a | 9,000 | 23,000 | 24,000 |
| | Carbon sequestered ($/year) | n/a | $205,000 | $524,000 | $547,000 |
| | **Pollution** | | | | |
| | CO removed (metric tons/year) | n/a | 5 | 13 | 14 |
| | CO removed ($/year) | n/a | $7,500 | $18,900 | $19,700 |
| | NO$_2$ removed (metric tons/year) | n/a | 30 | 76 | 79 |
| | NO$_2$ removed ($/year) | n/a | $299,300 | $754,100 | $785,200 |
| | O$_3$ removed (metric tons/year) | n/a | 93 | 235 | 244 |
| | O$_3$ removed ($/year) | n/a | $923,000 | $2,324,000 | $2,420,000 |
| | SO$_2$ removed (metric tons/year) | n/a | 3 | 7 | 7 |
| | SO$_2$ removed ($/year) | n/a | $6,600 | $16,600 | $17,300 |
| | PM$_{10}$ removed (metric tons/year) | n/a | 42 | 105 | 110 |
| | PM$_{10}$ removed ($/year) | n/a | $276,700 | $697,100 | $726,000 |
| | Total pollution removal (metric tons/year) | n/a | 170 | 440 | 450 |
| | Total pollution removal ($/year) | n/a | $1,500,000 | $3,800,000 | $4,000,000 |

[a] Urban land is based on population density and was delimited using the United States Census definitions of urbanized areas and urban clusters.  [b] Community land is based on jurisdictional or political boundaries of communities based on United States Census definitions of incorporated or census designated places.  [c] Urban or communities is land that is urban, community, or both. Communities may include all, some, or no urban land within their boundaries.  [d] Canopy green space is the tree canopy cover divided by total green space.  [e] Total green space (TGS) is total area − impervious surface cover − water.  [f] Available green space (AGS) is total green space − tree canopy cover (if the calculated value is less than 0, then value set at 0).

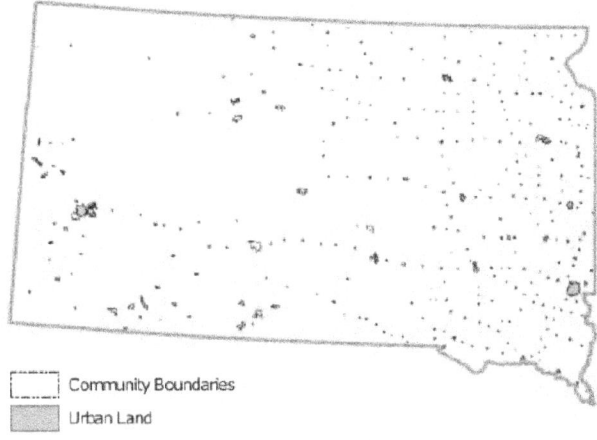

Community Boundaries
Urban Land

Figure SD-1.—Urban or community land in 2000; urban area relative to community boundaries.

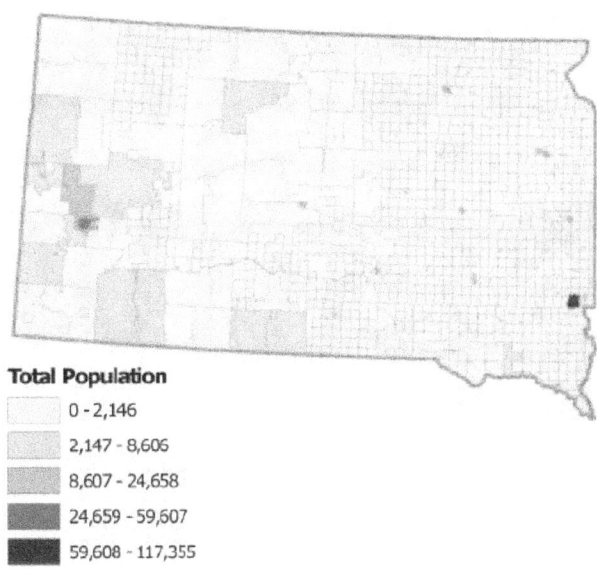

**Total Population**

| | |
|---|---|
| | 0 - 2,146 |
| | 2,147 - 8,606 |
| | 8,607 - 24,658 |
| | 24,659 - 59,607 |
| | 59,608 - 117,355 |

Figure SD-2.—2000 population within county subdivision boundaries.

## Human Population Characteristics and Trends

The population in South Dakota increased 8.5 percent, from 696,004 in 1990 to 754,844 in 2000 (Table SD-1). In South Dakota, 51.9 percent of the State's population is in urban areas (Fig. SD-1), and 71.6 percent of the population is within communities (Fig. SD-2).

## Urban and Community Land

Urban land comprises 0.2 percent of the land area of South Dakota, while lands within communities make up 0.8 percent of the State (Fig. SD-1). Between 1990 and 2000, urban area increased 9.8 percent, while community land increased from 0.7 to 0.8 percent (Table SD-1). Urban area in South Dakota is projected to increase to 1.0 percent by 2050, based on average urban growth pattern of the 1990s (Nowak and Walton 2005). Both urban land (attaining minimum population density) and community land (political boundaries) increased from 1990 to 2000. The percentages are calculated using the total (water and land) area of the geopolitical units derived from U.S. Census cartographic boundary data. Percent urban land varied across the State (Fig. SD-3; Tables SD-2 through 4).

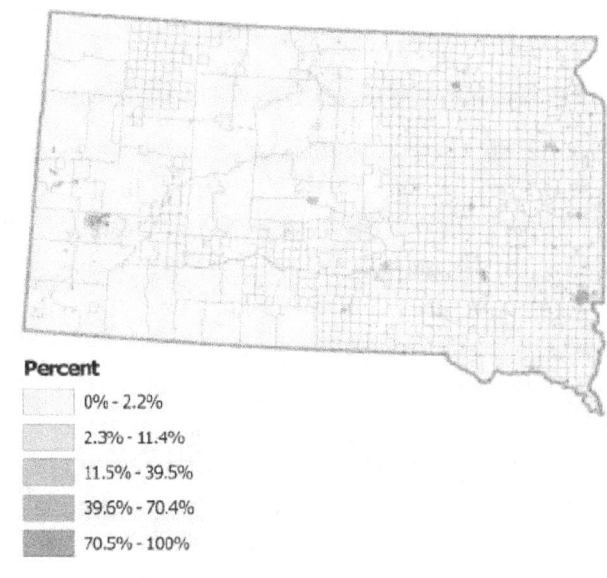

**Percent**

| | |
|---|---|
| | 0% - 2.2% |
| | 2.3% - 11.4% |
| | 11.5% - 39.5% |
| | 39.6% - 70.4% |
| | 70.5% - 100% |

Figure SD-3.—Percent of county subdivision area classified as urban land in 2000.

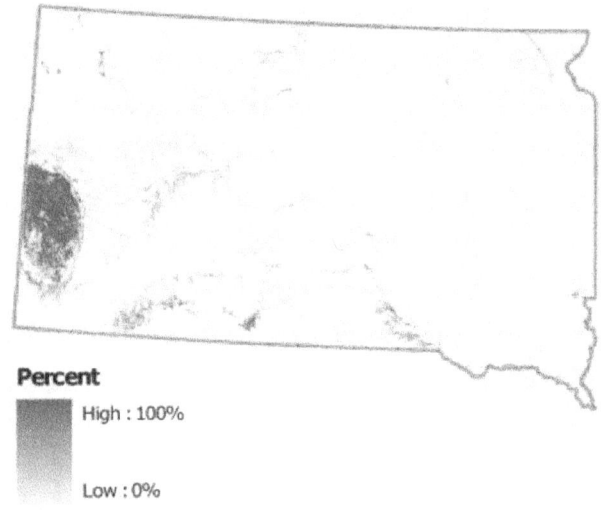

**Percent**

High : 100%

Low : 0%

Figure SD-4.—Percentage tree canopy cover.

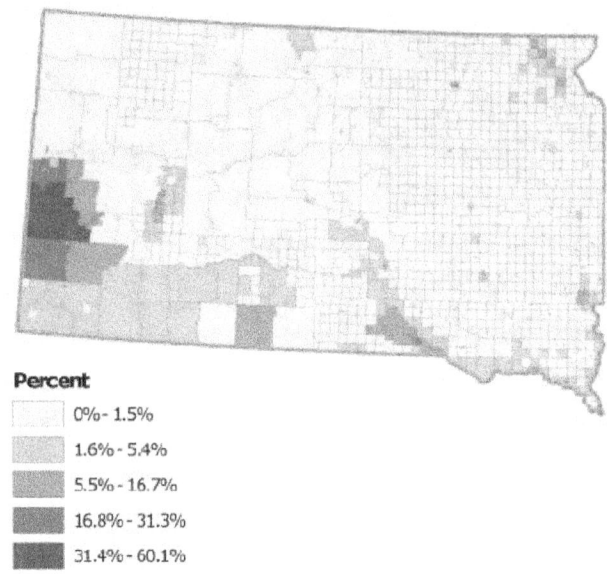

**Percent**

| | 0% - 1.5% |
| | 1.6% - 5.4% |
| | 5.5% - 16.7% |
| | 16.8% - 31.3% |
| | 31.4% - 60.1% |

Figure SD-5.—Percentage tree canopy cover within county subdivisions.

## Tree Canopy Cover Characteristics

Tree canopy cover in South Dakota averages 2.3 percent (Fig. SD-4), with 99.6 percent total green space, 2.3 percent canopy green space, and 5,875.3 $m^2$ of canopy cover per capita. Average tree cover in urban areas in South Dakota was 6.9 percent, with 72.8 percent total green space, 9.5 percent canopy green space, and 76.6 $m^2$ of canopy cover per capita. Within community lands in South Dakota, average tree cover was 4.6 percent, with 87.1 percent total green space, 5.3 percent canopy green space, and 139.8 $m^2$ of canopy cover per capita (Table SD-1). Tree canopy cover, canopy green space, and tree cover per capita varied among communities, county subdivisions, and counties (Fig. SD-5 through 6; Tables SD-5 through 7).

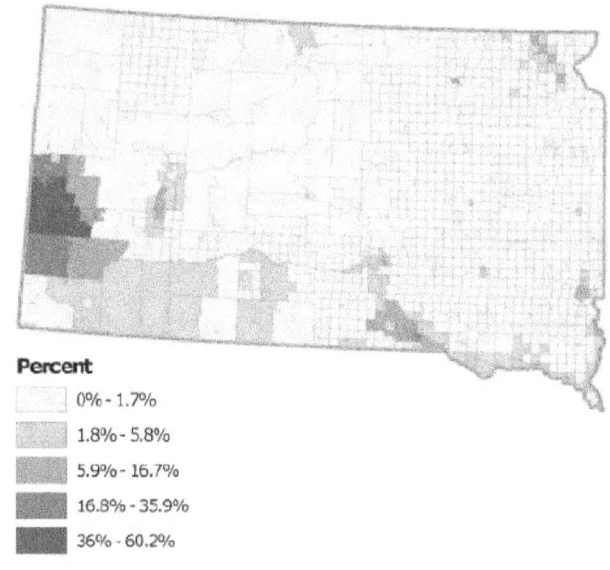

**Percent**

| | 0% - 1.7% |
| | 1.8% - 5.8% |
| | 5.9% - 16.7% |
| | 16.8% - 35.9% |
| | 36% - 60.2% |

Figure SD-6.—Percentage tree canopy green space in county subdivisions.

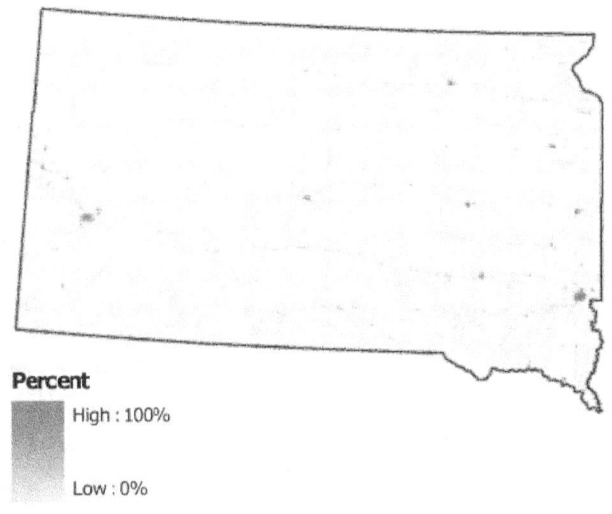

**Percent**

High : 100%

Low : 0%

Figure SD-7.—Percentage impervious surface cover.

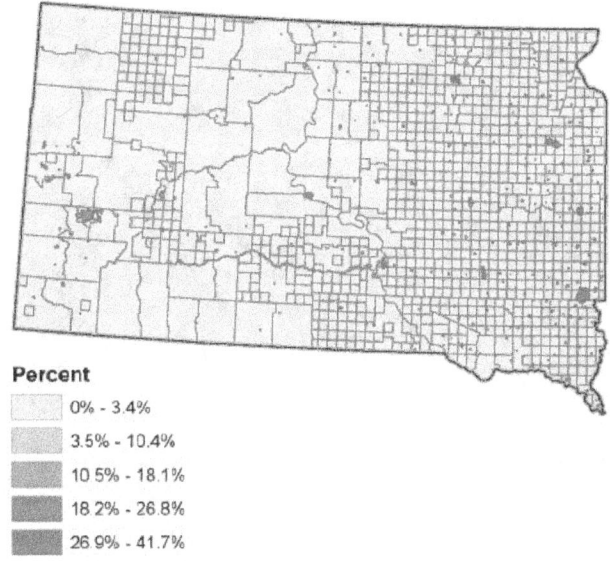

**Percent**

☐ 0% - 3.4%

3.5% - 10.4%

10 5% - 18.1%

18 2% - 26.8%

26 9% - 41.7%

Figure SD-8.—Percentage impervious surface cover within county subdivisions.

## Impervious Surface Cover Characteristics

Average impervious surface cover in South Dakota is 0.4 percent of the land area (Fig. SD-7), with 949.2 $m^2$ of impervious surface cover per capita. Average impervious surface cover in urban areas was 27.2 percent, with 300.6 $m^2$ of impervious surface cover per capita. Within community lands in South Dakota, average impervious surface cover was 12.9 percent with 392.6 $m^2$ of impervious surface cover per capita (Table SD-1). Impervious surface cover varied across the State (Fig. SD-8; Tables SD-5 through 7).

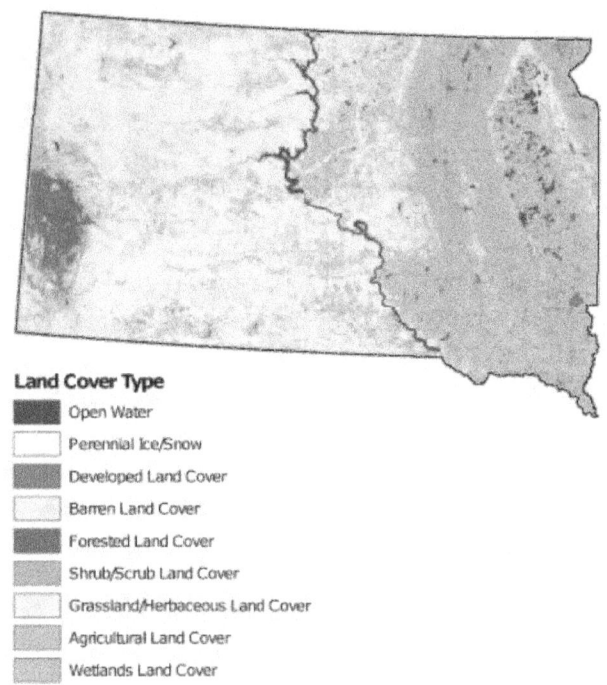

**Land Cover Type**

- Open Water
- Perennial Ice/Snow
- Developed Land Cover
- Barren Land Cover
- Forested Land Cover
- Shrub/Scrub Land Cover
- Grassland/Herbaceous Land Cover
- Agricultural Land Cover
- Wetlands Land Cover

Figure SD-9.—Classified land cover.

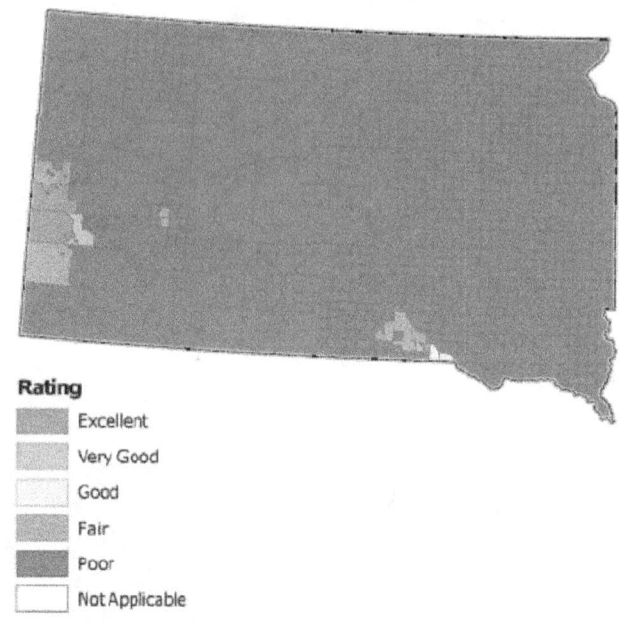

**Rating**

- Excellent
- Very Good
- Good
- Fair
- Poor
- Not Applicable

Figure SD-10.—Relative comparisons of tree cover for county subdivisions.

## Classified Land-cover Characteristics

South Dakota's land cover is dominated by grassland (Fig. SD-9). The characteristics as a percent of the total land area in South Dakota are (Tables SD-8 through 10):

- Grassland – 51.9 percent
- Agricultural – 37.7 percent
- Forested – 3.6 percent
- Developed – 2.9 percent
- Wetland – 1.7 percent
- Scrub/Shrub – 1.4 percent
- Barren – 0.9 percent

## Relative Comparisons of Tree Cover

Out of the 350 South Dakota communities, seven received a rating of excellent and 314 received a rating of poor (Table SD-12). Of the 1,361 county subdivisions, eight had a rating of excellent and 1,311 were rated poor (Fig. SD-10, Table SD-13); and out of 66 counties, two were given a rating of excellent and 53 were given a rating of poor (Table SD-14). Variability of assessment scores is a product of the difference in land cover distributions and the percentage of canopy cover within the population density classes and mapping zones (Fig. SD-10; Tables SD-11 through 14).

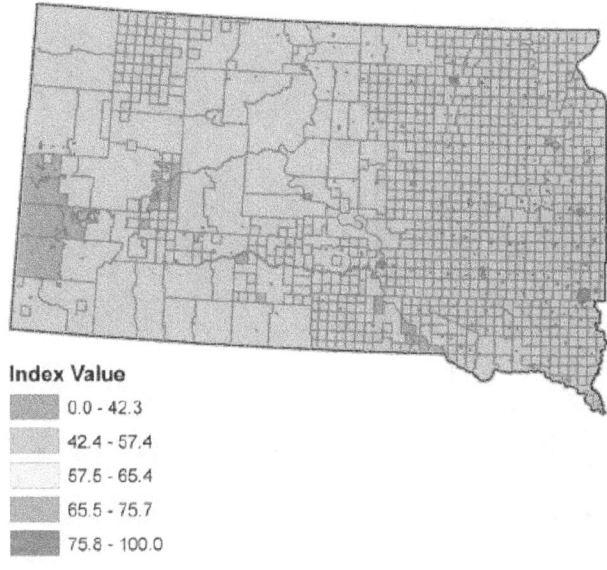

**Index Value**

- 0.0 - 42.3
- 42.4 - 57.4
- 57.5 - 65.4
- 65.5 - 75.7
- 75.8 - 100.0

Figure SD-11.—Planting priority index for county subdivisions. The higher the index value, the greater priority for planting.

## Priority Areas for Tree Planting

Priority areas for planting tend to be highest in more urbanized areas due to higher population density (Fig. SD-11; Tables SD-15 through 17). These index values can also be produced using high resolution cover data to determine local planting priority areas (e.g., neighborhoods).

## Urban Tree Benefits

The following forest attributes are estimated for the urban or community land in South Dakota (Table SD-1). These are rough estimates of values. More localized data are needed for more precise estimates, but these values reveal first-order approximations.

- 3.8 million trees
- 700,000 metric tons of C stored ($16.0 million value)
- 24,000 metric tons/year of C sequestered ($547,000 value)
- 450 metric tons/year total pollution removal ($4.0 million value)
  - 14 metric tons/year of CO removed ($19,700 value)
  - 79 metric tons/year $NO_2$ removed ($785,200 value)
  - 244 metric tons/year of $O_3$ removed ($2.4 million value)
  - 7 metric tons/year of $SO_2$ removed ($17,300 value)
  - 110 metric tons/year of $PM_{10}$ removed ($726,000 value)

## Summary

The data presented in this report provide a better understanding of South Dakota's urban and community forests. This information can be used to advance urban and community forest policy and management that could improve environmental quality and human health throughout the State.

These data establish a baseline to assess future change and can be used to understand:
- Extent of the urban and community forest resource
- Variations in the resource across the State
- Magnitude and value of the urban and community forest resource
- Urban growth in South Dakota
- Implications of policy decisions related to urban sprawl and urban and community forest management

# LITERATURE CITED

Dwyer, J.F.; Nowak, D.J.; Noble, H.M.; Sisinni, S.M. 2000. **Assessing our nation's urban forests: connecting people with ecosystems in the 21st century.** Gen. Tech. Rep. PNW-490. Portland, OR: U.S. Department of Agriculture, Forest Service, Pacific Northwest Research Station. 540 p.

Fankhauser, S. 1994. **The social costs of greenhouse gas emissions: an expected value approach.** The Energy Journal. 15(2): 157-184.

Greenfield, E.J.; Nowak D.J.; Walton, J.T. 2009. **Assessment of 2001 NLCD percent tree and impervious cover estimates.** Photogrammetric Engineering and Remote Sensing. 75(11): 1279-1286.

Homer, C.; Huang, C.; Yang, L.; Wylie, B.; Coan, M. 2004. **Development of a 2001 national land cover database for the United States.** Photogrammetric Engineering and Remote Sensing. 70(7): 829-840.

Homer, C.G.; Gallant, A. 2001. **Partitioning the conterminous United States into mapping zones for Landsat TM land cover mapping.** Unpublished U.S. Geologic Survey report. http://landcover.usgs.gov/pdf/homer.pdf. (1 August 2008).

Homer, C.; Dewitz, J.; Fry, J.; Coan, M.; Hossain, N.; Larson, C.; Herold, N.; McKerrow, A.; VanDriel, J.N.; Wickham, J. 2007. **Completion of the 2001 national land cover database for the coterminous United States.** Photogrammetric Engineering and Remote Sensing. 73(4): 337-341.

Murray, F.J.; Marsh, L.; Bradford, P.A. 1994. **New York state energy plan Vol. II: issue reports.** Albany, NY: New York State Energy Research and Development Authority.

National Climatic Data Center. 2000. **Integrated surface hourly observations 2000.** Silver Spring, MD: U.S. Department of Commerce, National Oceanic and Atmospheric Administration. [CD-ROM].

Nowak, D.J. 1993. **Compensatory value of an urban forest: an application of tree-value formula.** Journal of Arboriculture. 19(3): 173-177.

Nowak, D.J. 1994a. **Atmospheric carbon dioxide reduction by Chicago's urban forest.** In: McPherson, E.G; Nowak, D.J.; Rowntree, R.A. Chicago's urban forest ecosystem: results of the Chicago urban forest climate project. Gen. Tech. Rep. NE-186. Radnor, PA: U.S. Department of Agriculture, Forest Service, Northeastern Research Station: 83-94.

Nowak, D.J. 1994b. **Urban forest structure: the state of Chicago's urban forest.** In: McPherson, E.G; Nowak, D.J.; Rowntree, R.A. Chicago's urban forest ecosystem: results of the Chicago urban forest climate project. Gen. Tech. Rep. NE-186. Radnor, PA: U.S. Department of Agriculture, Forest Service Northeastern Research Station: 3-18 and 140-164 [appendix].

Nowak, D.J.; Crane, D.E. 2000. **The Urban Forest Effects (UFORE) model: quantifying urban forest structure and functions.** In: Hansen, M.; Burk, T., eds. Integrated tools for natural resources inventories in the 21st century, proceedings of the IUFRO conference; 1998 August 16-20; Boise, ID. Gen. Tech. Rep. NC-212. St. Paul, MN: U.S. Department of Agriculture, Forest Service, North Central Research Station: 714-720.

Nowak, D.J.; Crane, D.E. 2002. **Carbon storage and sequestration by urban trees in the United States.** Environmental Pollution. 116(3): 381-389.

Nowak, D.J.; Crane, D.E.; Stevens, J.C. 2001a. **Syracuse's urban forest resource.** In: Nowak, D.J.; O'Connor, P., comps. Syracuse urban forest master plan: guiding the city's forest resource in the 21st century. Gen. Tech. Rep. NE-287. Newtown Square, PA: U.S. Department of Agriculture, Forest Service, Northeastern Research Station: 9-14.

Nowak, D.J.; Crane, D.E.; Stevens, J.C. 2006d. **Air pollution removal by urban trees and shrubs in the United States.** Urban Forestry and Urban Greening. 4: 115-123.

Nowak, D.J.; Hoehn, R.; Crane, D.E.; Stevens, J.C.; Walton, J.T. 2006a. **Assessing urban forest effects and values: Casper, WY's urban forest.** Res. Bull. NRS-4. Newtown Square, PA: U.S. Department of Agriculture, Forest Service, Northern Research Station. 20 p.

Nowak, D.J.; Hoehn, R.; Crane, D.E.; Stevens, J.C.; Walton, J.T. 2006b. **Assessing urban forest effects and values: Minneapolis' urban forest.** Res. Bull. NE-166. Newtown Square, PA: U.S. Department of Agriculture, Forest Service, Northeastern Research Station. 20 p.

Nowak, D.J.; Hoehn, R.; Crane, D.E.; Stevens, J.C.; Walton, J.T. 2006c. **Assessing urban forest effects and values: Washington D.C.'s urban forest.** Resour. Bull. NRS-1. Newtown Square, PA: U.S. Department of Agriculture, Forest Service, Northern Research Station. 24 p.

Nowak, D.J.; Hoehn, R.; Crane, D.E.; Stevens, J.C.; Walton, J.T. 2007a. **Assessing urban forest effects and values: New York's urban forest.** Resour. Bull. NRS-9. Newtown Square, PA: U.S. Department of Agriculture, Forest Service, Northern Research Station. 22 p.

Nowak, D.J.; Hoehn, R.; Crane, D.E.; Stevens, J.C.; Walton, J.T. 2007b. **Assessing urban forest effects and values: Philadelphia's urban forest.** Resour. Bull. NRS-7. Newtown Square, PA: U.S. Department of Agriculture, Forest Service, Northern Research Station. 22 p.

Nowak, D.J.; Hoehn, R.; Crane, D.E.; Stevens, J.C.; Walton, J.T. 2007c. **Assessing urban forest effects and values: San Francisco's urban forest.** Resour. Bull. NRS-8. Newtown Square, PA: U.S. Department of Agriculture, Forest Service, Northern Research Station. 22 p.

Nowak, D.J.; Noble, M.H.; Sisinni, S.M.; Dwyer, J.F. 2001b. **People and trees: assessing the U.S. urban forest resource.** Journal of Forestry. 99(3): 37-42.

Nowak, D.J.; Walton, J.T.; Dwyer, J.F.; Kaya, L.G.; Myeong, S. 2005. **The increasing influence of urban environments on U.S. forest management.** Journal of Forestry. 103(8): 377-382.

Nowak, D.J.; Walton, J.T. 2005. **Projected urban growth and its estimated impact on the U.S. forest resource (2000-2050).** Journal of Forestry. 103(8): 383-389.

Ottinger, R.L.; Wooley, D.R.; Robinson, N.A.; Hodas, D.R.; Babb, S.E.; Buchanan, S.C.; Chernick, P.L.; Caverhill, E.; Krupnick, A.; Fritsche, U. 1990. **Environmental costs of electricity.** White Plains, NY: Oceana Publications. 769 p.

U.S. Census Bureau. n.d. **www.census.gov.** (January 2007).

U.S. Department of Interior, Geologic Survey. 2008. **Multi-resolution land characteristics consortium.** www.mrlc.gov. (1 August 2008).

U.S. Department of Labor Bureau of Labor Statistics. n.d. **www.bls.gov/ppi/** (June 2007).

U.S. Environmental Protection Agency. 2003. **National air quality and emissions trends report: 2003 special studies edition.** Research Triangle Park, NC: U.S. Environmental Protection Agency, Office of Air Quality Planning and Standards, Emissions Monitoring and Analysis Division.

U.S. Environmental Protection Agency. n.d. **www.epa.gov/oar/data** (June 2008).

Walton, J.T. 2005. **An investigation of national tree canopy assessments applied to urban forestry.** Syracuse, NY: State University of New York, College of Environmental Science and Forestry. 95 p. Ph.D. dissertation.

Yang, L.; Huang, C.; Homer, C.G.; Wylie, B.K.; Coan, M.J. 2003. **An approach for mapping large-area impervious surfaces: synergistic use of Landsat-7 ETM+ and high spatial resolution imagery.** Canadian Journal of Remote Sensing. 29(2): 230-240.

Zhu, Z. 1994. **Forest density mapping in the lower 48 states: a regression procedure.** Res. Pap. SO-280. New Orleans, LA: U.S. Department of Agriculture, Forest Service, Southern Research Station. 11 p.

# APPENDIX

## Urban Forest Data: States of the North Central West Region

The following tables are generated to support state reports on urban and community forests of the North Central West states of Iowa, Kansas, Minnesota, Missouri, Nebraska, North Dakota, and South Dakota. For specific state data tables use the CD accompanying this publication and search within the regional or state folder, or go to: http://www.nrs.fs.fed.us/data/urban.

## State Specific Tables:

**Table 1.**—Statewide summary of population, area, population density, tree canopy and impervious surface land cover, and urban tree benefits in urban, community, and urban or community areas.

**Table 2.**—2000 population characteristics, population change (1990-2000), and percent of land classified as urban within communities.

**Table 3.**—2000 population characteristics, population change (1990-2000), percent of land classified as urban or as communities within county subdivisions.

**Table 4.**—2000 population characteristics, population change (1990-2000), percent of land classified as urban or as communities within counties.

**Table 5.**—Tree canopy and impervious surface cover characteristics by community.

**Table 6.**—Tree canopy and impervious surface cover characteristics by county subdivision.

**Table 7.**—Tree canopy and impervious surface cover characteristics by county.

**Table 8.**—Land area, tree canopy cover, and available green space distributed within generalized land cover categories for communities.

**Table 9.**—Land area, tree canopy cover, and available green space distributed within generalized land cover categories for county subdivisions.

**Table 10.**—Land area, tree canopy cover, and available green space distributed within generalized land cover categories for counties.

**Table 11.**—Statistical summary of mapping zone values used to calculate urban and community forestry assessment.

**Table 12.**—Urban and community forestry assessment by community.

**Table 13.**—Urban and community forestry assessment by county subdivisions.

**Table 14.**—Urban and community forestry assessment by counties.

**Table 15.**—Planting priority index for communities.

**Table 16.**—Planting priority index for county subdivisions.

**Table 17.**—Planting priority index for counties.